PERFECT DESIGN

USING MATHEMATICS AND GEOMETRY TO BUILD GREAT LANDSCAPE DESIGNS

How to Forever Think Differently
about Visual Design

Richard G. Starshak

ISBN 978-1-63844-176-2 (paperback)
ISBN 978-1-63844-177-9 (digital)

Copyright © 2020 by Richard G. Starshak

All rights reserved. No part of this publication may be reproduced, distributed, or transmitted in any form or by any means, including photocopying, recording, or other electronic or mechanical methods without the prior written permission of the publisher. For permission requests, solicit the publisher via the address below.

Christian Faith Publishing, Inc.
832 Park Avenue
Meadville, PA 16335
www.christianfaithpublishing.com

Printed in the United States of America

Dedicated to…

Every backyard gardener, weekend planter, and dedicated landscaper who loves to get into the dirt and plant, yet wishes to design and build a better landscape.

Contents

Preface 13
Introduction 15
Chapter 1:   Mathematical Beginnings 17
Chapter 2:   A Brief History of Gardening 22
      European Gardening 24
      American Gardening 25
Chapter 3:   What Design Is 28
Chapter 4:   When Concept Becomes Design 30
      Seven Fundamental Tenets 30
          1. Design is the Answer. 30
          2. Design is a Priority Process. 31
          3. Design is Arranging Functions. 32
          4. Design Fills Three Basic Needs. 32
          5. Design with Real Goals. 33
          6. Design is Tools, Pieces, Principles, and Goals. ... 37
          7. Intricate Design is not Complicated Design. ... 37
Chapter 5:   The Three Languages of Visual Design 39
      1. Language of Principles 40
      2. Language of Functions 42
      3. Language of Selection 44
      How Designers Think 46
Chapter 6:   Let's Design! 48
      Vision 49
      Arrangement 49
          1. Creating Space 50
          2. Creating Impact 56
          3. Creating Stability 59

Selection 70
    Plants for Focal Points 72
    Plants for Framers 73
    Plants for Unity 73

Chapter 7:   Principles of Landscape Design 77
    1. Purpose 78
    2. Order 78
    3. Balance 79
    4. Harmony 79
    5. Interest 81

Chapter 8:   Applying Mathematics and Geometry to
                Landscape Design Principles 84
    1. Contents > (Total Space x 80%) 85
    2. Structure = (Order + Balance) 88
    3. Focal Area = (Space – phi) 88
    4. Focal Area > (Left Frame + Right Frame) 89
    5. Arrangement > Selection 89
    6. Impact > (Interest + Variety) 90
    7. What things do > What things are 90
    8. Elements > One Function 90
    9. Variety = (Square footage/8 to 12) 93
    10. Repetition > All other Attributes to Create
         Unity and Harmony 95

Chapter 9:   Specific Mathematical Applications to the
                Landscape 99
    1. Spatial Geometry 99
    2. Angles 108
    3. Geometry of Structure 118
    4. Focal Point Positioning 128
    5. Framers 133
    6. Harmony 133
    7. Interest 134

Chapter 10: Numbers Matter 136

Chapter 11: The Tools of Landscape Design 137
    1. Lines *are edges that pull your eye.* 137
    2. Color *plays with your emotions.* 138
    3. Texture *makes it appear as though you were touching it.* 138
    4. Form *gives shape with depth.* 138
    5. Numbers *mathematically affect us.* 139
    6. Order *establishes the rules.* 139
    7. Balance *places the axis line(s).* 139
Chapter 12: Ten Steps to a Great Landscape Design! 140
    Quick Notes 140
    Ten Steps to a Great Landscape Design! 140

Table of All Figures

Figure 1-1 Mathematical contributions from Greece 18
Figure 1-2 The golden ratio throughout history 20
Figure 2-1 BC examples of gardening..23
Figure 2-2 Common Era examples of gardening........................23
Figure 2-3 Designers and gardeners of the 1600s.......................25
Figure 5-1 Landscaping by Principles 41
Figure 5-2 Landscaping by Function 43
Figure 5-3 Landscaping by Selection 45
Figure 5-4 How designers think 47
Figure 6-1 The Design Process 48
Figure 6-2 Initial Bubble Diagram..53
Figure 6-3 Large Bubble Diagram 54
Figure 6-4 Step one of drawing the diagram 55
Figure 6-5 Step two of drawing the diagram 55
Figure 6-6 Step three of drawing the diagram 56
Figure 6-7 Increasing the impact of a tree....................................60
Figure 6-8 Two framers of the same variety
    around a focal point 62
Figure 6-9 Unifying underplanting...62
Figure 6-10 Helping a weak focal point..62
Figure 6-11 Trees framing a house...63
Figure 6-12 Example of framers too far apart..............................63
Figure 6-13 Examples of framers of focal area............................63
Figure 6-14 Using groups of three around a building to
    create structure...65
Figure 6-15 Establishing structure with groups of three................66

Figure 6-16 Example of good structure 66
Figure 6-17 Using groups of three to create structure 67
Figure 6-18 Using five elements to build structure 67
Figure 6-19 Using fives for structures. 68
Figure 6-20 Using groups of five in perennial beds 69
Figure 6-21 Example of selection around a garden 69
Figure 6-22 Example of a misplaced emphasis 71
Figure 6-23 Example of a misplaced emphasis 71
Figure 6-24 Example of a misplaced emphasis 72
Figure 6-25 Building interest through grouping 74
Figure 6-26 Examples of achieving impact 75
Figure 8-1 Fuller beds just look better 86
Figure 8-2 Filling the space that borders create 87
Figure 8-3 Example of elements having multiple functions 91
Figure 8-4 Example of elements serving more than one function 91
Figure 8-5 Example of larger landscape with elements
  serving more than one function 92
Figure 8-6 Examples of variety 93
Figure 8-7 Harmonizing with grasses 97
Figure 8-8 Harmonizing with perennials 98
Figure 9-1 Informal shape of the ellipse 101
Figure 9-2 Informal shape of a *peanut* 102
Figure 9-3 Tree placement with the golden ratio 103
Figure 9-4 Placing a shrub beside a house using the golden ratio 104
Figure 9-5 Pond placement in yard using the golden ratio 104
Figure 9-6 Bench placement in landscape bed using the
  golden ratio 105
Figure 9-7 Using the golden ratio to position a pond
  beside a large deck. In addition, the golden
  ratio is used to align the steps. 106
Figure 9-8 The golden ratio used for tree placement 107
Figure 9-9 The golden triangle 108
Figure 9-10 Angles and circles 109
Figure 9-11 The golden ratio revealed in circles 110

Figure 9-12 Using a golden triangle to place trees 111
Figure 9-13 Example of right angles providing structure.............111
Figure 9-14 Using strong 90-degree angles in garden bed 112
Figure 9-15 Using 45-degree angles with 90-degree angles
 along a wall 113
Figure 9-16 The golden angle in a round bed 113
Figure 9-17 Estimating angles of curves.......................................114
Figure 9-18 Aesthetically pleasing angles 115
Figure 9-19 Using the golden ratio to create pockets 116
Figure 9-20 Creating *softer* angles using the golden angle...........117
Figure 9-21 Creating structure with geometry 118
Figure 9-22 Building structure with single objects 119
Figure 9-23 The golden sections in a landscape 120
Figure 9-24 Building structure with triangles..............................121
Figure 9-25 Building structure with triangles..............................122
Figure 9-26 Using the points on the Fibonacci triangle to
 create structure 123
Figure 9-27 Deck and tree placement using the Fibonacci
 triangle 124
Figure 9-28 The Fibonacci triangle used to place three elements 125
Figure 9-29 Backyard layout using Fibonacci segments...............126
Figure 9-30 Using Fibonacci segment to place steps on desk.......127
Figure 9-31 A potential porch layout using Fibonacci
 segments for placement 127
Figure 9-32 Single-tree placement with golden ratio...................130
Figure 9-33 Two-tree placement using the golden ratio 131
Figure 9-34 Three-tree placement using golden ratio..................132

Preface

It is pure design, in its finest hour, that establishes the foundation of all matter at all times. Nothing exists, moves, lives, or dies without an order of design and underlying purpose. Design guides. Design works. Design rules. The history of the universe, the world, the separation of the waters, land, and air all lie in the mathematical construction of the basic building blocks of existence. Every electron, neutron, atom, molecule, and all living cells point to an orderly and mathematical design. The left-brain analytical and functional aspects of design combine with its right-brain copartner of visual order, arrangement, beauty, and aesthetics to provide a world of discovery, application, and aspiration!

Introduction

Welcome to the world of design. In as much as we see design encapsulate every aspect of life, we hold it somewhat reverently and with a definite sense of awe. It is easy to sense the design behind the arts, sculpture, materials, wood or metalworking, tools, machinery, buildings, cars, airplanes, rockets, and everything ever thought of, figured out or made in all of human history.

This book will affirm the vast utilization of principles of design, specifically visual design, and then add depth and breath to every aspect of that design world. We will look at the use of fundamental mathematical and geometric applications, thought more traditionally for building and engineering, and see how exciting it is to use these principles in building aesthetics into visual design based on numerical relationships.

This is a different approach to the study of landscape design. We will emphasize the mathematics and aesthetical geometry of design. This is a workbook about purpose, placement, proximity, numbers, structure, and ratios and how to utilize various tools and concepts to create visual unity, impact, order, balance, and interest. We will refer to color, size, texture, and such as needed; however we are emphasizing the mathematical basis of the visual design and not the individual characteristics and attributes of any particular elements within that design. We have included many sketches and landscape designs to guide you through this adventure.

Get ready to explore the great historical mathematicians and garden designers as they combine their resources, discoveries, and methodologies in an exciting and ongoing quest to build perfect design!

CHAPTER 1

Mathematical Beginnings

Mathematics and geometry surround us with fascination as they should and from the earliest times of recorded history. Even in the earliest records, we see counting and measuring (Samaria 3100 BC), a ten-number mathematical system in use (Egypt 2700 BC), geometric tables established with mathematical problems noted (Samaria 2600 BC), fractions and algebraic equations (Babylon 1700 BC), and a decimal numbering system with place value in practice (China 1200 BC).

We can look far back in the historical records and find among many things writings about squares and rectangles, the illusive problem of the square root of two (India 800–400 BC), and the use of rows and columns (China 700–600 BC). The Greeks and their far-reaching quest for wisdom contributed a large volume of mathematical and geometric knowledge. With the Greeks and their culture, the world gained the insights of a vast array of mathematicians, philosophers, composers, and astronomers.

We see incredible mathematical contributions from Greece over a few hundred years with the following:

Thales (624–546 BC)	Theories and triangles
Pythagoras (570–495 BC)	Geometric squares and triangles
Hippasus (500 BC)	Irrational numbers
Zeno of Elea (490–430 BC)	Infinity
Hippocrates (470–410 BC)	Summarized past principles
Democritus (460–370 BC)	Fractions, columns, and cone shapes

Mathematical Beginnings

Plato (428–318 BC)   Platonic solids, geometric proofs
Aristotle (384–322 BC)   Logic and mathematical reasoning
Euclid (300 BC)   Proofs, postulates, and axioms
Archimedes (287–212 BC)   Shapes, infinites, and value of pi

Figure 1-1 Mathematical contributions from Greece

With knowledge deepening, we see one generation building upon the previous generation, adding pieces of knowledge, expanding on what has been discovered, and stepping into the new frontiers of how mathematics and geometry reveal the design construction of the world around us. There is so much foundation, structure, and possibilities found in the numbers around us that every generation, from time long ago until today, shares in the excitement of new discoveries.

Finding the relationship between the diameter and the circumference of a circle or discovering the formula of finding the length of the far leg of a right triangle probably gave as much excitement as Fibonacci's writings of the sequence such named after him (1200s); factoring, trigonometry, and analysis of pi (1300s); trigonomic functions (1400s); natural logarithms, Luca Pacioli's Divine Proportion and imaginary numbers (1500s); analytical geometry and John Wallace's development of calculus (1600s); Newton's infinitesimal calculus and infinite powers (1700s); descriptive geometry, probability, quadratic reciprocity, prime numbers, least squares analysis, hyperbolic geometry, and elliptical functions (1800s); sets, graphs, probability, differential geometry, geometric topology and a myriad of mathematical truisms, proofs, and ah-ha moments (1900s); and a never-ending list of ever expanding theories, revelations, proofs, and applications (2000s)!

Our fascination is heightened when we can see application of such principles. As far back as 2725 BC and the construction of the Great Pyramid, we can observe various angles, ratios, and measurements. Although a multitude of conclusions have been drawn over time about the construction, some commentaries for and against such knowledge and application, it would be indeed difficult to argue against all such geometric applications being of just chance and lacking a knowledgeable basis in such a major construction.

We see that the ancient cultures of Egypt, Greece, India, China, and throughout the Middle East used geometric principle in the design and construction of various buildings, temples, and mosques as well as in other ornate artifacts in which to adorn them.

It would be difficult to imagine a culture not utilizing even the simplest of geometric principles to divide and lay out parcels of land, ownership and use, sizes of houses, courtyards, orchards and gardens, even a wall.

Pragmatism and application were more evident in the Egyptians and Babylonians, lacking recorded evidences of any fundamental rules or proofs. Trial and error of what works, with even close approximations for answers, seemed to suffice. There may have been the underpinnings of mathematical interests simmering in the world, especially in Greece; but it was not until the Greek Thales of Miletus (500 BC), considered by some to be the father of geometry, was credited with the first use of deductive reasoning and geometric principles.

It was Thales who mandated that reasoning with proofs was superior to experimentation and further showed proofs of right angles, triangular base angles, congruent triangles, and the bisection principles of a circle.

The architecture of the times was not shy about using such knowledge either. The aesthetics of geometry was permeating the culture. The pyramidal construction alone stands as a testimony of workable geometry, as the building of the Parthenon and multitudes of other examples. The greatest of all discoveries might be that of **"aesthetical geometry,"** that of the golden point or a particular point of measure on a line. It was that visually pleasing point that divided a line in two parts, whereas the ratio of the longer segment of the line to the shorter segment was equal to the ratio of the entire length of the line to the longer segment. This visually mysterious point fell at 61.803% of the entire line (0.61803), leaving the smaller segment at 38.197% (0.38197). Thus, 0.61803 (longer)/0.38197 (shorter)

Mathematical Beginnings

= 1.61803. And the entire line (100%) gives us 1.00/0.61803 = 1.61803!

We are left in a quandary of why this resonates with us so well. Why does this provide such a visual comfort? Why hold a mathematical ratio in such high esteem? Somehow this division of a line, in an area, in a painting, building, sculpture, or garden/landscape emanates a visual aroma and a soothing *aah* in our brains. Be that as it may, we see this golden point, or section, woven into many a work:

Phidias 384–322 BC	Used in Sculptures
Plato 300 BC	Recorded the use of this ratio
Euclid 287–212 BC	Wrote of the exact division of a line at this very particular point dividing it into its "extreme and mean" ratio
Fibonacci 287-212 BC	Wrote of the property of this ratio found within the sequence named for him

Figure 1-2 The golden ratio throughout history

It was Luca Pacioli (1446–1517), who wrote *The Divine Proportion* (1509), that stouts this special spot in the design world. Imagine something as simple as locating the point of emphasis in such a location that it would increase the aesthetics of the composition, increasing its interest, and creating a mathematical answer to a visual problem! Leonardo da Vinci (1452–1519) first called this the Divine Proportion and exemplified it in his most famous painting, *Vitruvian Man*. Martin Ohm (1792–1872) first coined the term *golden section*. Mark Barr (1871–1950) first used the term *phi* to apply to this special ratio.

It was also the astronomer Johannes Kepler (1571–1630) who stated that geometry has two great treasures. One was the Pythagorean Theorem and the other being the *golden ratio*. It was not in a bubble either that this beautifully positioned proportion could be applied broadly within the particular and practical architectural construction as well as in the arts, sculptures, drawings and paintings, and other representations of human life.

A view of such architectural drawings several centuries BC show the detailed points of arcs, ratios, squares, and particular points of intersection and placement to ensure maximum aesthetical value. And it was the detailed drawings of right angles, triangles, arcs, golden ratios, squares, and rectangles with their accompanying measurements that held the aesthetics in place!

On one hand, the foundations of mathematics and geometry were being established with aesthetical perspective walking ever more closely with the numerical functional analysis. On the other hand, we see the historical side of gardening/landscaping continuing to grow and develop. At some points, the two areas came ever so much closer together in their fullness. And for today? How awesome to have a set of guiding principles and mathematical influences to guide us in designing a garden or landscape!

Chapter 2

A Brief History of Gardening

If we can venture back in history far enough, we would observe that the very first evidences of *gardens* were those called forest gardens providing for the cultivation and harvesting of plant-based foods. These were gardens of necessity, of which we know quite little, although ruling out any particular aesthetic value altogether would be presumptuous at best. We cannot simply assume that there was no design basis at all since obviously there were rows, heights, borders, fences, or possibly a somewhat nice entrance for someone to arrive at the garden spot. Creating symmetry in some way or fashion would be quite likely and expected, especially in viewing the historical records of a world assembling mathematical equations and visually pleasing applications quite evident even as far back as 3500 BC.

We cannot know the depths of gardening, more likely small farming, back into history. Yet we know that food production beyond single-family gardening was also a necessity. Records from the Egyptian culture (3500 BC) reveals somewhat of the extent of their agriculture, with extensive designs complete even with the construction of their irrigation system. In the mid-2000s BC, Egypt, China, Peru, Crete, England, and others were well engaged in community gardening and farming.

In Egypt, we see pictorial evidence in paintings found in tombs dated at about 1500 BC. Palms and other such plants accompanied these pictorials of plants in aesthetical settings around ponds of water. In Persia (550–330 BC), we see evidences of a number of gardens, with the Persian influence venturing into Greece as noted by various writings of the gardens in the Academy of Athens, Theophrastus, and

Perfect Design

others. Gardens were quite evident in Rome at the villas of its more prominent citizens with topiary, water features, and other pieces of garden art placed throughout.

There is no lack of examples of the aesthetics of gardens long before the Common Era. In 1167 BC, Ramses III enjoyed his temple gardens. The Assyrians (900–612 BC) were tremendous gardeners. Following them were the Babylonians and notably Nebuchadnezzar II who flourished within the confines of the great Hanging Gardens of Babylon, an incredible wonder of the ancient world.

Persia was the next in line of dominant cultures, also with quite the love of the gardens. It was Darius the Great (521–485 BC), for example, who enjoyed his Paradise Garden of Persia. We also can see in this time period:

Aristotle (384–322 BC)	Kept his botanic garden in Athens
Theophrastus (Approx. 300 BC)	Wrote the History of Plants and Theoretical Botany
Epicurus (341–271 BC)	Recorded his walks in the garden
Emperor Wu-ti of China (Approx. 300 BC)	Had his extensive imperial garden

Figure 2-1 BC examples of gardening

It was just over 2,000 years ago that Vitruvius of Rome wrote his *Ten Books on Architecture* (27 BC), which included design, function, architecture, aesthetics, and landscaping. In the Common Era we have records of the following:

Rome (Approx. 250)	Agriculture, horticulture, livestock, and botany
China and Japan (Approx. 400)	Mountains, water, and rocks as parts of the garden
Arab World (Approx. 600)	References to walls, foundations, and mosaics
Hindu and Arabic (Approx. 760)	Used math with decimals to track costs, prices, and materials

Figure 2-2 Common Era examples of gardening

European Gardening

It was in the late 1200s that the Europeans began to have an increased desire for the more aesthetical pleasure of the gardens, yet until about 1500, we still see most European gardens of any stature attached to monasteries or the manor house. These were common to be enclosed having fences, walkways, raised beds, and an abundance of herbs.

The 1500s had their own excitement about the gardens, flush with Italian renaissance influence, as the knot garden among other things was introduced. More architectural features found themselves within the confines of the garden with fountains and even a garden house. Cultivating flowers for their beauty was perfectly acceptable!

The 1600s saw the size of the more affluent gardens grow with added terraces, walkways, and topiaries. We see the influence of Greek and Roman design ushered in as there arose a more focused approach to presentation utilizing proportion, balance, and symmetry, with definite lines of axis, crossing paths, and emphasis on square- and rectangular-shaped planting beds. Also in vogue was statuary, mazes, and nice new assortments of vegetables!

The European gardens of the 1700s to mid-1800s was privy to more of the park-like settings: lots of shrubbery and less formal design. Public gardens were created in London. The Society of Gardeners began in England in 1725.

The Victorian age (1830s–1900) was marked by a turning back to a somewhat more formal style with bright colors and exotic plantings. There was a higher degree of plant collecting resonating in the garden world. Glass houses just for plants came into use. Gardens saw rocks and boulders as respectable additions to the presentation to bring forth heightened interest. And by 1900, here we go again. We saw a turning back to the more informal.

Famous gardeners/designers were well respected and employed in the 1600s and 1700s, among them were the following:

William Kent (1685–1748)	Redesigned the gardens at Chiswick (1731) and worked on the design at the Roushum Garden
Charles Bridgeman (1690–1738)	The royal gardener for Queen Anne and Prince George of Denmark

Figure 2-3 Designers and gardeners of the 1600s

Both of these designers championed the melding of the formal with the informal in order to portray the best of both "gardening worlds."

Possibly the most well-known gardener of the day was Lancelot Brown (1716–1783). Recognized as England's greatest gardener in the day and designer of some 170 parks, he heralded the view, contrary to many, that the garden should be natural, almost native, and somewhat indistinguishable from how nature is arranged in and of itself. Almost as well-known was Humphry Repton (1752–1818) who saw a marked shift against the informal as the tide was swaying back once again to a more formal garden layout.

American Gardening

In the Americas, the early colonists established their gardens in much the same manners as in their home countries. Colonial garden substance and technique saw little in the way of design change, structural improvements, or horticultural changes between 1600 to about 1775, even extending into the early 1800s. Garden *how-to* books were written not by the Americans but by Europeans. However, seed exchanges were of a fluid level as numbers of newer varieties of seeds were sent back to the European continent. The colonists received generous amounts of seeds in return from many sources and areas, even as far away as China. The colonists were also quite proficient in the growing of fruit trees, flowers, and herbs.

Design seemed to take place more by necessity. Typical gardens might be raised squares with a pathway from the house, herbs and more popular cooking plants nearer to the house, but no plantings by the house. Garden size was more dictated by family size, with style resulting somewhat from location: more formal settings in New York, Boston, or Philadelphia and less so in the more rural country settings.

There is some research that indicates that the colonists had a lower tolerance for vegetables, more so for grains and meat. However, when the first true American garden book was published written by John Randolf (1760s), he used ample pages discoursing on the growing of a variety of vegetables as well as herbs.

Although the early 1800s saw the formation of the Horticultural Society (1804) in England, most American gardens remained functional, food producing, and practical—*kitchen gardens*, as they were called. However, there were prominent exceptions such as Thomas Jefferson's home and garden estate in Monticello (1820s) or Maplewood Gardens in Ontario and British Columbia (1830s).

The mid-1800s were a different kind of entity altogether as gardening was slowly becoming a leisure activity. So much so that we see the kitchen veggie garden diminishing and the ornamental garden begin to rise in prominence. Researchers introduced new varieties, garden-care products, fertilizers, and preventatives.

Andrew J. Downing published *A Treatise on the Theory and Practice of Landscape Gardening* (1841) and *The Fruits and Fruit Trees of America* (1845) and began publishing *The Horticulturist* magazine (1845). Frederick Law Olmstead provided design to New York's exquisite Central Park (1859) along with designer Calvert Vaux, with input from the popular garden writers John and Jane London.

Thomas Meehan (1826–1901), a well-respected horticulturist, wrote *The American Handbook on Ornamental Trees* (1853) insisting that a tree belonged in every landscape. Alice Earle (1853–1911) writes of the necessity to *enclose* the garden by either walls, fences, or hedges. Neltje Blanchan (1865–1918) emphasizes getting design help and assistance, just as one does with their house. Grace Tabor

(1872–1972) stresses foundation lines. Create the skeleton…the pattern!

By the late 1800s the *garden* was being relocated out of the front yard to its new home in the back of the house, and America was flush with books, writings, magazines, and ideas for crops, gardens, horticultural applications, and landscape presentations. We were seeing the combination of horticultural relevance and aesthetical significance in showcasing both the leisure aspect and the design aspect in the garden/landscaping composition.

The Victorian age of gardening in Europe (1830s–1900) was certainly walking closely with its American counterpart. What an exciting moment in American history to see such incredible growth stemming from the intellectual and the compositional melding of the design process. Aesthetical relevance is seen in the design process. The selection of particular plants and other pieces of art and objects in the garden/landscape were highlighted to be seen. Presentation was for the more astute viewer. Uniqueness was welcomed.

The 1900s saw an explosion of garden and landscape theory and principles. Marjorie Cortley (1892–1954) wrote in detail of the principles of color, hues, and values with its various uses in complementary or contrasting arrangements. Garrett Eckbo (1910–2000) wrote in explicit terms of structure and spatial perspective, as well as extensive explanation of mass and form, texture, and the partnership of arrangement and selection in a design.

Chapter 3

What Design Is

At the very core, design is simply a plan showing an overall concept or function, how parts are arranged and interconnected, to meet a specific need, object or aesthetical view. For us in the world of landscape design, we see design as a visual composition in which the arrangement shows purpose, unity and balance with some variety, uniqueness or interest. There are indeed many different fields of design as engineering, mechanical, medical or architectural. In the visual realm we see painting, sculpture, various forms of art and of course landscape design. Comprehending the mathematical or the geometrical application of these is paramount to establishing the visual design. What do we mean by these terms?

> **Mathematics**—The study or science of numbers, order, quantities, space, and measurements and the relationship of such numbers to each other and the subsequent results.
>
> **Geometry**—Within mathematics, it is the study of points, lines, angles, and shapes and their relationships to each other, within two- or three-dimensional objects.

We will also establish the premise that landscape design is both a functional and visual answer to a particular outdoor visual problem. Yes, we can provide a **strictly functional** (although partly visual since we do actually see it) design as seen in the design of, for example, an automobile engine: functionally correct and visually understandable in the arrangement of the parts, its use, its sustainability and its repair. Little visual aesthetics are resonating here.

Urban planning can also be highly functional in many ways: managing traffic and pedestrian patterns and separating commercial and residential areas, as well as designating areas for community services, utilities, and entertainment or shopping areas. All of this does not require an aesthetical side to it but only the ability to comprehend the connectedness of its parts to the whole and understand its functional layout and use.

Design can also focus on the **visual for visual's sake**. Most often, we see this in the counter cultural portrayal of art—*modern* art or *new* art lying somewhat outside aesthetics' nurturing arms and set before the viewer's discretionary eyes of self-interpretation. This lacks the principles that hold it together and simply supplies the viewer with an instant pop of color, texture, size or form—the immediate impact of dissonance in one visual way or another.

Chapter 4

When Concept Becomes Design

As a concept, landscaping becomes a design when the one who draws becomes the designer. It is the deeper, fuller, richer understanding and comprehension that injects the designer with insight (instant discernment), perception (sensitivity), intellect (fundamental principles), and wisdom (application over time). It is in this understanding that designing is a multitude of orderly concepts that will establish and confirm the cognitive opus within the mind and thoughts of the designer.

Seven Fundamental Tenets

Here we have gathered seven fundamental tenets of understanding what good design is and how designers can raise their comprehension level and application:

1. Design is the Answer.

It is the design that is needed—an order of arrangement of particular pieces in relation to one another, in correct proportion, assigned a function with a unified final presentation. Design is not a picturesque garden or pieces of a magazine page, a bit of impact with splashes of color to make it interesting. Design is the correct arrangement of the pieces within a space, based on principles of composition that will result in both the final use of that space and an aesthetical value resonating out of it.

2. Design is a Priority Process.

Good design results from an orderly process in and of itself coupled with a hierarchy, a priority, which looks like this:

VISION ➡ ARRANGEMENT ➡ SELECTION ➡ RESPONSE

(knowing that…)

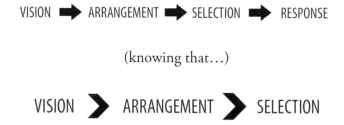

Simple as it seems, this order is critical in the design process. It is easy to sway and wonder how we might *design in* good aesthetics, which is quite impossible outside of keeping things in order.

Vision is king! Vision drives the entire design process, tells us where we are going, and delivers a picture ahead of time as to what this will look like when complete!

Arrangement is the actual and perceived interrelationship of all the parts in a unified final presentation. It tells the "story" of why this garden or landscape exists. It can be intricate but not complicated, simple to perceive but also interesting in the mind.

Selection is the choosing of what the real and actual pieces within the composition will be. It is here that most consideration will be made to color, texture, height, movement, sound, and smell. This is not a geometric decision but an aesthetical decision. The full understanding of this lies in this basis: good arrangement may be able to overcome a poor selection; however a good selection will never overcome a poor arrangement! Looking for good aesthetics? Write this in stone:

Good vision leads to good arrangements
(geometric relationships and patterns).
Good arrangements leads to good aesthetics!

3. Design is Arranging Functions.

This is not to be confused with the functional analysis in the site plan where each area has a designated function and which is well needed. This is the understanding that *each and every piece* in the landscape has an actual, identifiable purpose and function. The designer will see each piece first and foremost for what it is *doing* (focal point/emphasizer, framer, unifier, filler, etc.) in the arrangement and then secondly what each piece actually *is* (maple tree, hydrangea, hosta, bird bath, begonia, etc.).

The designer will see the landscape design as structure, background, focal point, primary left framer, secondary right framer, unifier, filler, and so on, naming each piece by function. Thus the boxwood, for example, in this particular design at this point is a left framer; the smaller hydrangea on the other side is a secondary right framer. The variegated hostas are unifiers/harmonizers, and the coral bells are fillers. The pieces are set into the composition with the correct numbers, locations, ratios, and proportion/scale.

4. Design Fills Three Basic Needs.

Although a landscape may seem to have many different applications, it will help if we really see the three encompassing reasons that a landscape truly exists. This will help us focus on what the visual answer has to be, not what it may drift off to become. These reasons are the following:

A. To warm or soften an area

This is the simple foundation plantings along the house, a small bed somewhere by the patio or deck or a few perennials along the driveway or front walk. They are not meant to be overwhelming or intended to make the viewer stop and linger over their beauty. They are truly filling a nice little space. Small spaces are not big into entertainment!

B. To hide an area

Nice big shrubs, evergreens, tall grasses, and such go here; but no color, focal points, garden art, unique plantings, or your special 22-inch hanging basket. We do everything we can to cover and run. The last thing we want to do here is catch the eye and pull it in over, so keep it blah but a bit in order.

C. To highlight an area

These are your larger perennial beds, the berms, the big wide beds in front or back of the house, theme gardens, the place where you often sit and relax, the water garden, the dozen containers on the patio, or the window boxes. Bring on the arrangements, impact, color, and more!

5. Design with Real Goals.

Visual design will use geometric tools to represent specific *pieces* guided by *principles*. At times, we raise the continence of these principles as if they were the goals themselves, such as "We are looking for perfect balance" or "We need to make sure that unity is the main thing." In these statements, we have just substituted a principle for a goal. Unity, as well as balance, order, purpose, harmony, and interest are principles, not goals. Centering, highlighting, framing, and such are assigning functions to various pieces. These are the techniques of applying proportion, perspective and scale, and such to correctly place these pieces throughout the composition, not necessarily achieving the goal.

These are the actions and the motions that will provide good aesthetics, which will in turn achieve the real goal—the feeling, the continence, and the satisfaction emulating from the complete garden or landscape presentation. I love the cognitive levels that design provides us—a gift of the creative process. We humans simply love to create, to process, to be challenged, and to figure it out. We want to attain that very real sense of personal accomplishment.

Three Design Moments We Love

As we dig even deeper into this very lively enterprise of creating something, we can discern its unique characteristics that draw us in, hold us there, and then bring us to that level of fulfillment. This ultimate goal is actually three-fold:

A. In-The-Moment Designing
B. Owning-The-Moment Designing
C. Completing-The-Moment Designing

A. In-The-Moment Designing

It is this time in the design process that initiates and sustains the entire cognitive interweaving that takes place as we create. We see it plainly when we are creating *something*. This may be a monthly planner, a trip, an activity, a project, or a landscape. We enjoy the challenge of it, and we do not wish to rush through it. That is the first indication that we have entered the gate of *design-time creativity*.

This is that time we are nicely focused at the project at hand, highly into our right-brain creative and imaginary or artsy design mode, in which we are quite content to be actively engaged in the process. We do not necessarily want the project to come to an end too quickly! These moments are highly stimulating, and as designers, we live for them!

We also know that we are there when we do not want to solve the problem or accomplish everything all at once. It is the changing of the pieces, the functions, the views, and the possibilities that intrigue us and keep us focused at the task at hand. We may lose track of time, slow down our time frame, or even be quite satisfied at *working on it* but not quite finishing it.

We see it also when we are *working out* and implementing the design we just mentally and visually created. We definitely see it as gardeners. How often do we want to work outside in the gardens for the afternoon? Who cares how long it takes? We are enjoying the time. We want the moment to last!

As an occasional jogger, I sense that moment as I warm up a bit at first but then settle into a rather nice rhythm for the rest of the route. The very best time is when I first begin to sense that rhythm—the time when I am starting to work my plan and the moment where I am in the zone but have the rest of the run to go. I am not in much of a hurry to finish the course or the time.

B. Owning-The-Moment Designing

There is a dramatic shift from enjoying someone else's work to enjoying my own work. Although one may enjoy the art museum immensely, there is a different level of contentment and satisfaction in delighting in the work of our own hands. How espousing and gratifying to be able to say that you envisioned, you planned, you designed, and you built it! Ownership has its own level of excitement, and it certainly takes one's own project to a deeper level of satisfaction.

Ownership can arise very early in the process; the difference of implementing someone else's landscape plan verses our own originality. As designers, we should recognize it when we first grasp a vision, the concept of the construction process, and the manner of expression through the arrangement of the pieces within the landscape. Ownership is with us all the way to the end as we respond to the intricate work of our own hands. We are much privy to this in the landscape design process as we create purpose, theme, impact, variety, and interest within our own personality. It is this second conceptual part in the design process that truly excites us because our own stamp of ingenuity is imprinted in our own outdoor compositions!

C. Completing-The-Moment Designing

As humans—as designers, builders, and accomplishers—we all desire to have a sense of completeness and finality. There is an emptiness when we do not or cannot complete the process. We do not like unfinished closets, bathrooms, painting jobs, or landscapes. Just like jogging, at some point, no matter how much in shape, the vision changes to being done. We want to cross that mental finish line, take a shower, get a sandwich, and watch some TV. We want the reward for completing the task we set before us.

This is vision's end product and the realm of accomplishment that is the ultimate goal of the designer. And as well-grounded and highly attuned designers, we understand that these are the morsels of aesthetic satisfaction that greet us at the finish line. Designers design for design's sake. Designers are mentally prepared to see things in terms of the mathematics and the geometry within any visual arrangement set before us. Designers analyze things beyond the landscape because design is set within everything we see. Design is meant to be perceived. We as designers apply the insight, knowledge, and wisdom we attain and take it to the end. It is then the comfort, peace, tranquility, emotions, the understanding of the design, and the comprehension of how it works—as a whole, as pieces, as a statement, and as its unity—which provide the ultimate fulfillment. We ourselves were created to enjoy such moments!

It is amazing, however, that the very cognitive high that we ascertained in the design process is also a bit fleeting. Jogging is not a one-day event never to be done again. Neither is a painting, a project, a chore, or planning a highly creative event. We were made to create and to create again. Although I highly enjoy walking the newly landscaped beds here at the garden center, I find that after time I view them less—with less enthusiasm and with less creative analysis. But as gardeners and landscapers, we enjoy an advantage in that we do not have to begin anew every time that we wish to design anew. The artist, sculpture, metalworker, seamstress, and so on needs to start fresh with new material and media. We can return to our original pieces of work and endlessly renew, tweak, adjust, move plantings, borders, beds, and interest to recreate and recreate our compositions.

6. Design is Tools, Pieces, Principles, and Goals.

Each is separate, but just like a good composition, we will see harmony in these areas. Each piece needs to be accurately placed within the design, in scale and proportion. Penmanship and accuracy regulate the process. We need to make our drawings—especially if we hand draw, which is perfectly acceptable and less intimidating—look like the piece we are drawing. This is not where we use squares and triangles to represent shrubs and flowers! If we wish to be able to delineate and construct as a designer, we need to think like a designer as this pictures the process more accurately:

I'm going to use these: **Tools**	That represent these: **Real Things**	Following these guidelines: **Principles**	To get these results: **Goals**
Points	Edges	Purpose (reason, theme, vision, function)	Ambience
Lines	Borders		Comfort
Shapes	Fences		Peace
Proximity	Trellis	Order (arrangement, position)	Contentment
Variety	Trees		Pleasant
Space	Flowers		Feeling
	Ponds	Balance/Weight	Closure
	Shrubs	Unity/Harmony	
	Lawns	Interest/Selection	
	Walks		
	Art		

We work with tools to represent actual pieces, guided by principles to achieve a response.

7. Intricate Design is not Complicated Design.

In design, intricate is the correct and detailed combination of all the individual pieces, which may very well be a very large actual number of pieces. **Intricate**, within this natural progression of design, guided by principles, becomes very doable and exciting. By knowing where the concepts and precepts align within the design process, the designer rises to a better standing and posture, with a much better command of the competency and skillfulness of our craft.

When a visual composition is **complicated**, it is difficult to quickly grasp and discern. When a landscape is viewed, it is the unity that is first recognized, then the main impact/theme of the entire presentation with the structure and framing, the lesser individual subfocal areas with its framers, and then details and interest.

Multiple endings to the visual process are available to the storywriter/designer. But as with any literary prose, if too many subplots entangle the story line, it is ramping up the busyness of the main plot with irrelevant details. This simply does not work well.

Simple comprehendible concepts will bring recognizable order and direction to the landscape. Simplifying the understanding results in deeper immediate awareness. High perception is high quality design. Remember:

***Viewers are attracted to the presentation because of the impact.
They will stay for the interest.***

CHAPTER 5

The Three Languages of Visual Design

What is it that lifts our design abilities to that next level? What is it that takes what we know then applies it, but somehow we are still not reaching that emotional *in-the-moment* design high that we are looking for? We look at our work, and it just doesn't have the *pop* or the *uniqueness* that puts our stamp of ingenuity on it. Where is the depth of detail and understanding we are searching for?

If I had to choose a single concept that truly catapulted a designer forward, it would be this: that we tend to lean heavily on the selection process, even if we try to wait, and we tend to talk the language of **What-Goes-Where Landscaping.** This is the design that we put together both in our mind and on our paper, for yourself or your client, and shows what plant or other feature goes where. Somewhat rightly so are we drawn to this point, for who wants a landscape design that shows all of the underlying construction principles or the functions of all its pieces?

To be the designer that we want to be, we need to be submerged in the world of visual thought: concept, process, and construction of pure design—design for design's sake, as the early mathematicians did geometry for geometry's sake. No particular application was always in mind, often just the study of theorems or postulates for the intrigue and understanding it held. I know that I have done many a sketch just doodling on scratch paper, even when I should have been listening to something else! I had our garden center sketched out several times, considering different looks, long before we ever bought the property, just exploring a number of design what-ifs.

At the very core of cognately and cohesively putting this all together is the comprehension that designers are speaking different design languages at different times which look like and sound like these:

1. How things align—Language of Principles
2. Why things work—Language of Functions
3. What things are—Language of Selection

There is going to be some overlap between these concepts, as *interest*, for example, is used in more than one way; but they are still separate and distinct from each other in several ways. Grasping these different ways to describe the design process will sharpen us as we will better comprehend what is being discussed or analyzed, in what way, and where it fits into this process.

1. Language of Principles

These are the guidelines for visual relationships within a unified composition. They guide the process from start to finish. These are the words and concepts that hover around the arrangement of the elements and their relationship of size, distance, numbers, and proportion to each other. At the cornerstone of all design are the five principles of design:

Purpose—Order—Balance—Harmony—Interest.

When we are in the conversation and someone mentions balance, we know they are speaking principles, part of the overall order and structure within the arrangement. If they mention theme, we know they are speaking of purpose. If they wish to discuss the varieties of coneflowers, then they are talking about selection and interest. The following page shows what a design by principles would appear as.

Perfect Design

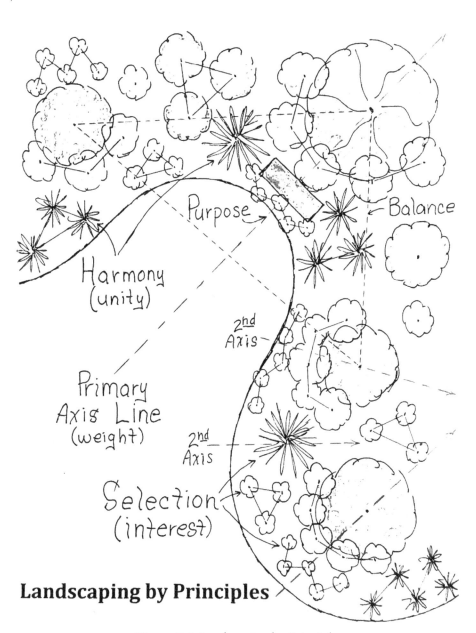

Figure 5-1 Landscaping by Principles

2. Language of Functions

This is a second and entirely different language. This specifically indicates what each piece in the landscape is *doing*, its role, and its job. This is less used than the application of principles yet is critical to understanding why the entire composition works. These are the words we often hear:

**Focal Point/Emphasizer—Framer—Unifier
or Harmonizer—Filler.**

As a designer, we need to be able to look at a design—or walk through a garden or landscape, even a fairly large one—and point to each and every piece and call it by its function. "That is a sub-focal point. That is a primary left framer. That is the secondary right framer. These are under framers. These are part of the focal area. That is a harmonizer, and that is a filler." We need to think, create, and analyze in the world of function, albeit very left-brain orientated. This helps us *build* the landscape, to *construct* its parts, and to *design* its operations. These are the words of parts, pieces, and jobs. We are the engineers of good design.

This is designing by function, which is very much different than the final copy we all wait to see where we show what every planting is, how many there are, and where they all go! But because we think as designers, we separate this from the final design. We set in place the functional aspects first. This is the size, shape, numbers, location, and the mathematics that guide such aspects. An example of what a functional landscape design looks like is on the next page.

Perfect Design

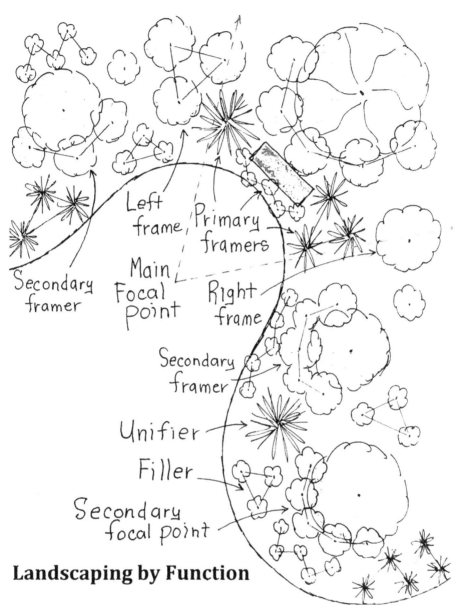

Landscaping by Function

Figure 5-2 Landscaping by Function

3. Language of Selection

This is our most comfortable language and what we use with the final design for ourselves or our clients. However, its roots are in the first two languages, and we would never arrive at this point if it were not for the groundwork already established. This moment is not possible without the core principles and functions set in place, whether we recognize them or even acknowledge them. Picking out random pieces, without direction, will likely result in a Tower of Babel in our backyard—confusion over what, where, and why things are where they are.

However, this is the most fun language to be immersed in for it is a language of visual attributes, details, and all sorts of interesting things! These are the words we use here:

Color—Size—Texture—Height—Movement—Sight—Sound—Smell.

Perfect Design

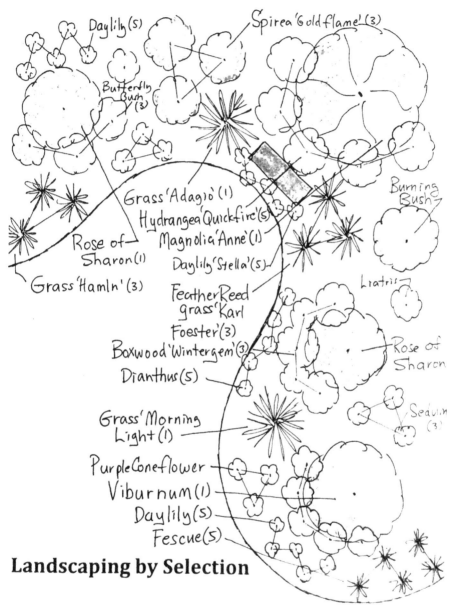

Figure 5-3 Landscaping by Selection

The Three Languages of Visual Design

How Designers Think

At this point, we will explore a bit on how designers think. Much emphasis has been devoted to **what designers think** as to an order or a process. It is much easier to consider what we do first, then second, and so forth. However, **how we think** considers the process itself versus primarily the final outcome of such thinking. Yes, we are looking at the final pieces—the trees, shrubs, perennials, containers, etc.; but the stimulating confirmation of where we are in the process, and why, is most invigorating and satisfying!

I remember so well our first real home after being married for ten years. It was a very simple bi-level, but it had a very nice sized lawn. I soon noticed that as I pushed the mower across the grass, I created lines in the lawn from the wheels. Although temporary, I found that I could make straight lines along strait walks and borders, ninety-degree angles at corners, softer lines around softer areas, and circles around trees. There was a very real enjoyment in the discovery that I wasn't just cutting the grass. I was presenting the lawn! Since we now had some flower beds, I soon learned the art of weeding and groundskeeping. That visual satisfaction again moved me, this time from weeding plants to showcasing perennials. And with my first real weed trimmer, I took great satisfaction, not in trimming, but in the craft of highlighting the borders. Slowly but surely, I was thinking as a designer. I was beginning to understand the process. I was seeing things differently. And after twenty-five years of designing landscapes, I still rest on those early moments of discovery!

Understanding the entire gamut of landscape design is where our study is leading us, and knowing where we are in that process is key to final construction and application of a great landscape design! **Designers think design!** To design better, we need to think better. To comprehend as a designer, we need to be able to separate the various parts and subprocesses that are interacting as the design is being constructed. The following chart summarizes the *pieces of the process* and how we comprehend and construct this process in our minds. This is conceptually how designers think:

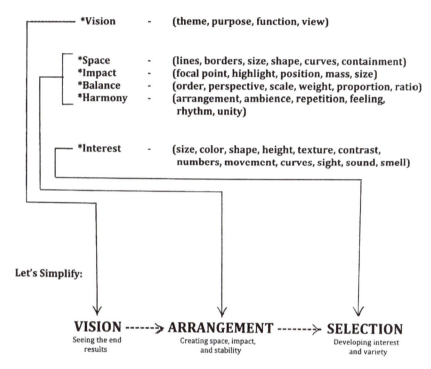

Figure 5-4 How designers think

Let's Simplify:

Chapter 6

Let's Design!

No doubt many a gardener/landscaper has begun a project, for example, to hide a fireplug. A few shrubs surrounding it really helped and maybe just a few dailies to make sure it wasn't overly drab or depressing, followed by a couple of little perennials that were on sale, and of course, we just couldn't resist the color of the geraniums we spotted. So they went in there too—along with the rock with our address on it!

Oh yes, the picture of that old fireplug eyesore is now the highlight in the front yard and somewhat more obvious than it was just a week ago. Of course the point being that in reality, it is easier than we think to get off track from the original plan we had in mind. Knowing that the process requires a plan in written visual form will at least make us commit up front to our original intent. Let's look at this **tried and true natural process** more closely as this is the very heart and soul of visual design. Staying in order truly does give incredible results:

Figure 6-1 The Design Process

Vision

All design, in every form, resonates from vision. This includes every type of business, organization, charity, community project, use of space, art, and landscape design. This is the mind's ability to picture it done: the overall look, basic structure, and, possibly but not necessarily, the details, varieties, and pieces of interest that would eventually be included. As we said earlier, clear vision drives the project forward from beginning to end.

Arrangement

This is the most challenging part of the process. It is more encompassing with more opinions and more advice than any other step. Entire books are written and devoted to the **principles of landscaping** that govern the placement and arrangement of a multitude of elements within a designated space. This is taking the concept that we wish to visually display with using all the pieces we want to somehow fit in, from trees and shrubs to favorite perennials and newest annuals, a walkway, bird bath, some mini boulders like the Johnsons have, and so on. All this needs to be set in some kind of order, where we like to see it from most often, balanced with other viewing spots and guided by a few mathematical principles!

Arranging the pieces to create a pattern, whether extremely simple (five shrubs in front of the house) or intricate (backyard cottage garden), requires a process in and of itself. As designers, we create something. Whenever we sketch an element into the design, we have just created something. As we draw the lines for our borders, we create space, enclosure, and our art board to work on within our artistic playground.

Within the step of arrangement, we see the life of the entire process. This is what I call the **Big Three**—the plan, the heartbeat, and the creation by the designer to put their own stamp on their imagination as far as one would go. It is the subprocess within the process of arrangement. Inside of the umbrella of *arrangement*, we see three actions: an area that needs to be designated, some emphasis added to give the area a purpose for being there, and some structure so that we can set *other things* into it where everything generally looks like it all belongs. That doesn't seem too hard. In simpler terms we are:

1. Creating *Space*.
2. Creating *Impact*.
3. Creating *Stability*.

Arranging is comprised of outlining or enclosing the space we will use and then highlighting an area to give some emphasis or theme. We add stability by including some structural elements that will hold it together, imply some age to the area, or simply frame in the more impactful areas of the landscape. It will be the principles of landscaping in the following chapter that will guide us through this *creative process*.

1. Creating Space

This is quite a critical starting point in the process to be certain. The creation of space should be quite esteemed within our visionary expectations. I see this mismatch from time to time. Recently I went to advise at a country home with a fairly large landscape area. It had been the same for years, and the couple was definitely looking more at retirement than not. As I was talking to the husband, it was obvious that the two of them never even considered changing or reducing the space. We talked and discussed the real starting point. "Let's look at how much space we are using, maybe we don't need this much." The more we talked about actually reducing the space, he finally admitted that he did not want to spend anywhere near the time he had been doing to keep up the maintenance. We hadn't even talked about the plants, yet he was already overjoyed at the new design they were about to implement!

There is definitely much more freedom today to create large and flowing landscape beds on all sides of the home. It is not uncommon in new home construction to build in large planting areas between the home and the sidewalk leading to the driveway. It almost assumes that this area needs to be filled, but this has led to more than one discussion of putting down a lawn in one-third or even one-half of this area and create a more manageable space to build a moderate-sized landscape.

What needs to happen in these somewhat larger and more intricate design possibilities is the discussion and analysis going back and forth between vision and space. "If we put a bed here what could we plant?" "What if we made this bed larger or shaped it differently, then what could we do with it?"

On the other hand, we also see the couple so engaged in the gardening, groundskeeping, tending the plants, moving, dividing, and rearranging. They just enjoy the outdoors and to be in their garden. They may very likely have a planting playground that is just too small for them. "How can we tell?" The easiest way is to sense the desire not to be done—they simply **do not ever want to be done**, even for one day. They want to be *In-The-Moment* (as we discussed), being fully part of a never-ending outdoor activity.

These are the folks who will constantly be weeding, moving stuff, replanting, changing the path, tearing something out, and putting something in. Why? They want to design something and then build it. And gardening is something they can handle, nurture, and see come to life. These are the people that simply need to add space. How much space? Here is as much an unbiased way to look at it as I can think:

Space allotted for gardens and landscaping should equal the area that will nicely challenge your time and talents, but not overwhelm you.

Designing is a desire nearly all of us have inside of us. Whether it is the simple crayon drawings of a youngster, making doll clothes, building a fort, doing a craft project, assembling a term paper, or rearranging the kitchen cabinets, it is designing. My recent task of cleaning out the garage quickly turned into something quite engaging when I decided to rearrange the work tables in there and then put it all back together in a somewhat different arrangement. I went from the chore of cleaning to the task of designing and was quite *In-The-Moment* for several hours!

As we dive into the world of *space*, it does not take long to recognize that this is quite an unexplored world. We consistently emphasize **filling the space** but much less consider **creating the space**. It is much more exciting to talk about the things arranged within such space than the absence of things—the hollow, the emptiness, and the nothing-allowed-in-here-yet area. This is thinking in the design world at its core, the concept of "What emptiness do I wish to contain in order to hold the specific things I wish to show forth?" This is the visionary moment that sets in motion our conceptual thinking and is as close to **design meditation** as we can get.

It is this back-and-forth rippling between vision and space (and its possible application) that works so well. We visualize. We then consider what space might work. We then go back to revisit our vision. We then go forward to consider if that space might work and so forth that makes this moment in the visual design process such a powerful duo!

As we match our space to our vision, we need to decide on what the space will actually look like. What geometric shape do we desire? After placement, based upon what we have already thought it would look like, we need to decide at least generally on a formal versus informal appearance. The formal design has the appearance of two matching or closely matching symmetrical sides. This type of arrangement utilizes more straight edges, right angles, matching pieces with typically a bit more of a manicured look to the plants and art. Informal design presents itself with more curves in the borders, softer angles, impact points not precisely centered, and more loosely balanced visual weight.

Formal arrangements will employ geometric shape within the space also, as squares, rectangles, or circles. We see free-flowing shapes within the outline of more informal presentations. Formal design suggests expectations, which are lower, for what we see on the left, we will indeed see on the right. Interest is limited. Informal design allows expectations to be surprising, and adding bits of interesting things will be easier.

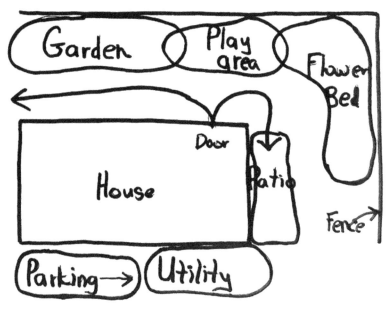

Figure 6-2 Initial Bubble Diagram

As we lay out an entire area, such as the entire property or the entire back yard, we will see multiple spaces created of various shapes and with possible overlap amongst them. These initial *bubble diagrams*, as they are known, show where the various functional areas lie. We then use these overviews and approximations to construct the more exact measurements and details of each individual space:

Figure 6-3 Large Bubble Diagram

At this point, we will begin to add a number of examples, sketches, and landscape designs. By choice, we will not use computer-generated presentations, but we will use simpler and easier hand-drawn illustrations. It can be somewhat or even highly intimidating

Perfect Design

to compare oneself with the output of the computer. Thus, we will utilize the same type of results that you will get when you sit down at your desk or kitchen table.

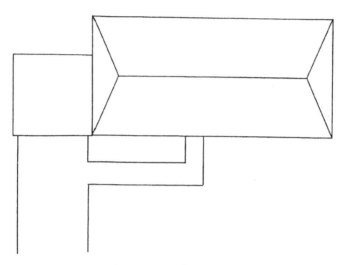

Figure 6-4 Step one of drawing the diagram

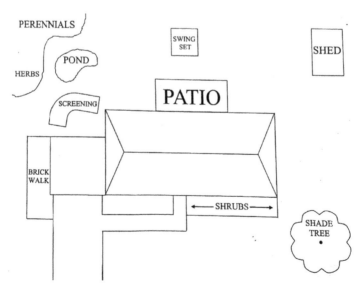

Figure 6-5 Step two of drawing the diagram

Let's Design!

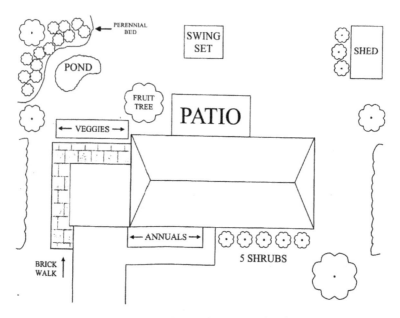

Figure 6-6 Step three of drawing the diagram

2. Creating Impact

The impact, emphasis, purpose, theme, or focal point is the reason the landscape area exists. It commands attention; stands out because of size, color, position, or prominence and is very easily identifiable. Impact lies within the broader structure of the entire surroundings we just created with our space. Yet at times, the structure is, or is a part of, the area of impact. Impact works with space. The reason a border arcs outwards (expanding the space) is for the purpose of *holding something* significant. It would not lay out the red carpet without something with a bit of emphasis jumping in. It is a tandem relationship between the two of them!

These pleasing points within the landscape are set apart as points of contrast between them and the rest of the nearby surroundings. A good test of impact is how quickly these points of emphasis are recognized, as well as other functions in the landscape. There is a definite pecking order to composition recognition, and if not readily seen as such, then every element is not working its job or working together. If we have to explain our landscaping, it is not working. The order of quick recognition is as follows:

Unity → Impact → Structure and Framers → Harmony → Fillers

Redesigning an area is not a failure; no one can nail it all down first time out. However, when we change something, we should be able to identify why it was not working well and how to correct it. I have no problem with calling something a **design error**—a mistake in placement, proportions, angles, a ratio, or a particular color or such. As a designer, we will need to make decisions for ourselves or a client and make the correction. This will help sharpen our skills as we analyze the composition. We need to correctly say, "The focal point is about 50 percent too small," or "The left secondary framers are too colorful," or "The axis line needs to move about a foot to the right." Analyzing a landscape presentation with "It just doesn't look right" is not acceptable.

Creating immediate impact and comprehending the concept of the landscape rises in importance as we elevate from smaller basic landscape designs to larger, more intricate or more personable gardens and landscapes. Planting a row of shrubs in front of the house (softening) does not require a strong central theme. However, as we build somewhat larger flower or perennial beds, bird gardens, sanctuary gardens, or memorial gardens, we need both a strong level of immediate impact and a good sense of adding the details, variety, and interest to support the entire aesthetical look.

Included on the following page is our **Hierarchy of Theme Gardens** that we employ here at the garden center. This gives a sense of design concentration needed to ensure that we quickly recognize a bird garden from a more broadly planted perennial garden or a more delicately mannered fairy garden.

Let's Design!

Theme Garden Hierarchy
Developed by the Garden Path Decatur, Il

Feelings	Prayer & Share Meditation Sensory	Healing Enabling Secret	Hideaway Fragrant Heirloom	Musical Biblical Sanctuary
Personalities	Hummingbird Container Apothecary Culinary Kitchen	Grasses Pizza Rose Herb Cutting	Sound Fairy Bird Butterfly Miniature	Fireplug Bed Frame Bowling Ball Touching Garden Art
Concepts	Rock Woodland Sitting Fruit	Cottage Pond Strolling Veggie	Fountain Wildflower Hosta Children's	Water White Japanese R, W, & Blue
Landcaping	Colonial Victorian Country Yard	Spring Summer Fall Hedge	Patio Entrance Driveway Romantic	Shrub Berm Three Season Low Maintenance
Beds & Borders	Annuals Perennials Walkway	Formal Informal Color	Corner Sunny Shady	Doorway Under Tree Flower Beds
Plantings	Shrubs	Flowers	Plantings	Foundation

3. Creating Stability

Good recognizable structure and easily identifiable repetition, either in the main pattern or just as a harmonizing element seen throughout the area, pulls the entire composition together and stabilizes it. Combining order and balance creates structure. It is this strong relationship that adds stability and holds the entire package in place. Structure utilizes **recognizable order (including background) and visual weight (including framers), along with adequate focal area and vertical vision.** It is the hearty bones of the landscape without the need to command any unique impact, recognition, or striking interest.

We can think of structure as something like this: it is the visual weight spread throughout the established space with minimal impact value. We want the viewer to quickly sense the unity that these particular pieces give yet not compete with the intended place of emphasis and purpose. These are the pillars in the theater, not stealing the show from the stage but simply adding visual strength and order to the presentation. Structure exists to add mass and volume—to fill the vertical space. It can lift the canopy. It encloses the space. Structure gives a sense of time and longevity. It gives strength and holds the space together by attaching the horizontal to the vertical.

By using the more systematic principle of order and combining it with the weightier principle of balance, we simply get good structure. This equation forms the basis of the architecture of the landscape: **Structure = (Order + Balance).**

Building Structure with Numbers

Structure can also be seen as part of the focal point when it is the **one main piece** in the landscape area, such as a single large tree. This is a challenging design in that we usually wish to highlight that which lies under the tree, such as the perennial bed or patio. The tree can overshadow the emphasis we wish to use below its branches. Formula-wise, we can do just two things. This provides a method for

Let's Design!

any time this situation occurs where the structure (which may be the primary framers) is simply too impactful and takes the impact from the focal area and lavishes it upon itself. We solve this design problem by applying one or both of the following two remedies:

1. **Increase the impact of the focal area**
2. **Decrease the impact of the structure (and framers)**

In this case where it would be impossible to reduce the height and volume of the tree, we can only increase the impact (size, color, position) of the focal area. Thus, in this case the answer would be to expand the size of the patio, and then fill it with things that are impactful (furniture, planters, containers, grill, garden art, and so on) until in appearance, it pulls the eye from the structural piece onto the focal area.

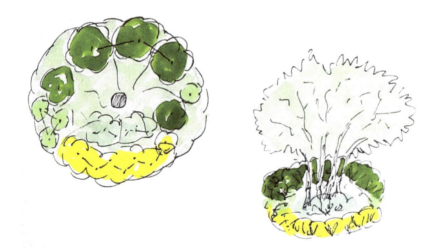

Figure 6-7 Increasing the impact of a tree

The **number two** is a special number with a special job. Its one and only job is to frame something in, to lie one on the left and one on the right of a particular piece that we wish to bring attention— somewhere between making sure a somewhat smaller subfocal piece of interest is seen or to show the way to the yard, to the front door, to the larger and quite stellar focal point, or to the large berm in the front yard.

We create stability by framing areas of impact, which help guide the eye as well as adding *weightier* pieces where one would expect them to be. Framers are matching, or near matching, elements placed at either side of another more prominent element which will visually indicate an area of emphasis, uniqueness, or recognition. Framers positioned tightly around the focal point, or even touching it, are immediate, primary framers. Framers positioned on either side on the focal area, but with other pieces or planting in between them and the focal point, are secondary framers. Plantings immediately in front of and shorter than the focal point are called under framers.

Left and right framers that are not matching are nonetheless still doing their job, not because of identity but because of position, owning their rightful spot within the composition. Thus, one larger shrub as the left frame is equal to the weight of three medium shrubs as the right frame. By geometric location alone, they are framers.

Two elements used to build structure will be seen as framers since two is a framing number. Its only function is to frame something else, something more prominent and impactful than themselves. Two elements, or pieces, build structure in this unique way; and if they are not doing their job, the design quickly weakens, even to the point of obvious visual dissonance.

Using only two pieces to build structure is nearly impossible. Either the two are so far apart in the area, two fifteen-feet trees for example, that the entire space in between them is technically in the focal area and visually are expected to be filled with some sort of emphasis. At times, the two framers are positioned to the immediate left and right of the focal piece, appear to be part of the focal area, but then leaving too much space between them and the end of the area. When structure relies on the framers, as in somewhat smaller landscape areas, it is best to include them as part of the focal area and

Let's Design!

then tie them in by under planting both the focal point and the two framers with a single variety planting as in these examples:

Figure 6-8 Two framers of the same variety around a focal point

Figure 6-9 Unifying underplanting

Figure 6-10 Helping a weak focal point

Figure 6-11 Trees framing a house

Figure 6-12 Example of framers too far apart

Figure 6-13 Examples of framers of focal area

Let's Design!

If framers are immediate and visually appear as part of the focal point, we simply refer to this as the *focal area*. If it looks like a duck, it is a duck. We can call anything by any name or function in the design layout, but **it is what it is perceived to be**. By designing, we should not encounter this problem. However, when we are consulting or analyzing a current and established landscape, we may very well encounter this situation. This is critical, as we shall shortly see, that we have the ability to name each piece in the landscape by function.

During a recent consultation, the homeowners, whom had a very lovely yard, recanted that visitors saw their gardens from the patio but never really ventured down to stroll them at close proximity. Although there were several areas where the borders came out to create a nice subfocal opportunity, it was centered with a rather small planting with a number of other plantings around it. In essence, it simply did not have a strong focal point at all. The viewers saw at a distance a mix of color and texture with little impact to pull them over. All the framing around the main planting was miniscule in proportion and was not part of the focal area at all. Neither were the under framers since there was very little matching or positioning to them. These beds consisted of, in actuality, a weak focal point and fillers only. Once they redesigned the areas and created impact with better framing versus planting something nice, the situation was much improved!

In another consultation, we reviewed a rather large crescent-shaped landscape area in a corner of the backyard. There were a couple of large trees on the backside, as well as some medium-sized shrubs throughout. There was also a fairly large tree on the far left but nothing on the right. This tree was prominent and nice looking. It was positioned as a possible subfocal point. However there was nothing to balance it out on the right, and the bed ended closer to the focal area on the right side also. By repositioning and extending the border which now included a similar planting on the right, it changed the function of the tree on the left. It was clearly now the left frame in the area and made the entire presentation multiple times better!

Perfect Design

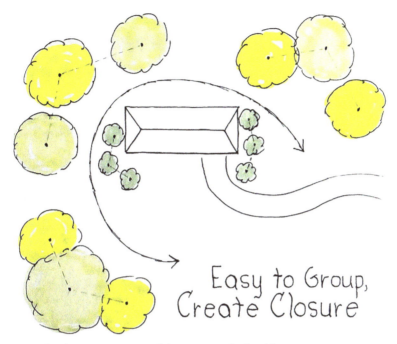

Figure 6-14 Using groups of three around a building to create structure

Using the **number three** for establishing the structure of the area adds a very strong visual statement as it is nature's highly respected and greatly esteemed near-perfect number. We see it everywhere in the design world and most definitely in the world of landscape design. The number three can represent three points, can imply a straight line, can bend to indicate closure of a particular area or portion of an area, or create an innumerable amount of triangles points (both formal and not) that show the triangular formation within an area. This visually triangular shape that it arrays can be used anywhere from major structural points to minor fillers between other more prominent plantings.

Let's Design!

These are examples of using this incredibly powerful number when establishing the bounds of structure:

Figure 6-15 Establishing structure with groups of three

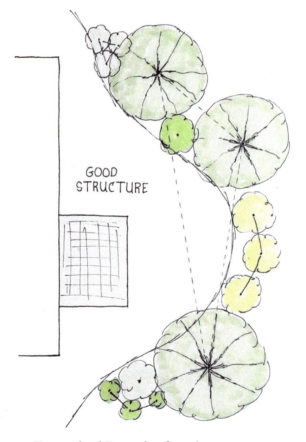

Figure 6-16 Example of good structure

Perfect Design

Figure 6-17 Using groups of three to create structure

The following are examples that use **five elements** in building structure. This is a great natural number to utilize in the design, as it can be set as a straight row, as a formal background, but can also zig-zag—three forward and two back or vice versa. We can more closely enclose an area with five pieces, even slightly curving one end in more than the other if we choose or even create a small tree line:

Figure 6-18 Using five elements to build structure

At this point in the process, we have stressed the importance of laying out a visual geometric structure in our design with respect to position, size, and numbers. We have gone from the original bubble layout, which should note both functional and aesthetical needs or wishes, and designed a plan showing the more exact location and relative sizes of the focal area/point, structural elements, and immediate and secondary framers.

Let's Design!

Figure 6-19 Using fives for structures.

It is in the **principles of design** where we will apply a closer look at numbers, ratios, and geometrically aesthetical placements. At this point, our premise is to show how we can establish a structural framework in which to set our impact, variety, and interest *into*.

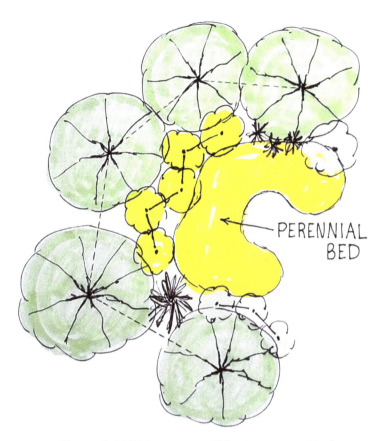

Figure 6-20 Using groups of five in perennial beds

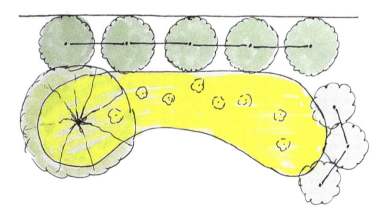

Figure 6-21 Example of selection around a garden

Selection

It is not that selection of all the plants and features is entirely separate from designing all the framework and structure of the garden/landscape. It is most common to have some degree of vision devoted to the actual plants, pieces, and art that will be eventually incorporated into the design. A shade garden most likely will have hosta in it. A bird garden will have a birdbath somewhere located, maybe as the centerpiece or maybe as a piece of art amongst the other plantings set somewhere within the broader theme of the designer.

It is here though that we choose the details. We have a vast array of garden possibilities and attributes such as size, color, form, height, texture, contrast, sight, sound, and smell. We are indeed limited by the space allotted to each element but very free within those parameters to fully enjoy the creative design moments we so passionately look forward to. Selection moves the eye by choosing (mostly) hotter colors for impact and quite often cooler colors for immediate framers. We see that hotter, brighter colors (white, yellow, red, orange, pink) will intensify impact and cooler colors will de-emphasize impact.

Contrasting colors, one next to the other, reveals an area of high change and brings the eye to where the action is. Variegated (two or three leaf colors) plants, which are easily spotted, will create quicker and more readily seen harmony. Plantings with other similar features will also add harmony with utilizing similar form or height, texture, or a particular number in a small grouping.

It is here that we need to look closer at particular plants, the *What-Goes-Where-Landscaping*. Particular plants, by the nature of their features (size, color, texture, etc.), lend themselves to specific functions. Boxwoods create nice backgrounds, foundation plantings, even framers; yet they lack any prominent features to really consider them as focal points. Long-blooming colorful roses or hydrangeas make for great impactful plantings but not great framers, as they will compete for the attention of the focal point thus creating friction as to where the eye should go.

Perfect Design

Figure 6-22 Example of a misplaced emphasis

Figure 6-23 Example of a misplaced emphasis

Let's Design!

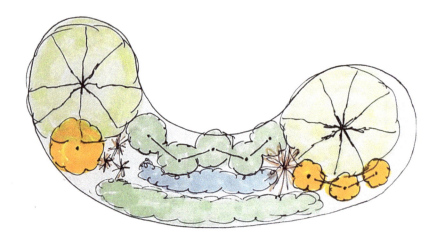

MISPLACED EMPHASIS

Figure 6-24 Example of a misplaced emphasis

Plants for Focal Points

Small Trees	**Shrubs**	**Perennials**
Japanese Maples:	Hydrangea	Heleopsis
Crimson Queen	Roses (various)	Black Eye Susan
Bloodgood	Dogwood	Cone Flowers
Coral Bark	(variegated)	Hibiscus
Hydrangea Tree	Viburnum	Russian Sage
Rose of Sharon Tree	Weigela	Yarrow (yellow)
Weeping Cherry	Rose of Sharon	Grasses (larger)
Weeping Norway Spruce	Topiary Evergreens	Coreopsis
Dogwood Tree	Buddleia (dwarf)	Honeysuckle Vine
Magnolia (dwarf)		Clematis Vine
Dwarf Alberta Spruce		Hosta (large or giant)

Table-1. Plants for focal points

Plants for Framers

Shrubs	Perennials
Boxwood	Coral Bells
Holly	Sedum
Euonymus	Daylilies (dwarf)
Spirea	Mounding
Yews (spreading)	Hostas (small or medium)

Table-2. Plants for framers

Plants for Unity

Grasses, liriope, hosta (variegated), coral bells (dark leaf), artemisia, and other variegated foliage plants or others when planted in groupings.

A most wonderful and popular gardener and writer, Penelope Hobhouse, uses many chapters in her book *The Cottage Garden* to guide her readers as to which plants should go where for what purpose and for what look. It is the eye of a good designer that differentiates and articulates the many particular elements available to obtain the maximum artistic visual relevance in the entire design presentation.

Remember, impact rules. A focal area of five hydrangeas with three dwarf shrub roses in front of them is fairly impactful, especially with a few more annuals in front of the roses. However, using two smaller hydrangeas for the left and right framers may be quite appropriate and aesthetically acceptable because they cannot possibly have enough impact to compete with the much larger and more colorful main focal area.

Interest is also **designed *into* the geometry** in several ways. First, we can alter the numbers of the framing plantings on each side of the focal point, as the one larger shrub on the left with the three medium shrubs on the right, assigning them equal visual weight. Secondly, we can consider alternating other plantings' and secondary framers' numbers. If we use the design above with one large shrub

Let's Design!

on the left and three medium shrubs on the right, we can then place three somewhat smaller plantings on the left and one bit larger planting (matching the weight of the new threesome on the left) on the right. Alternating ones and threes on each side of a middle area is an easy way to assign some degree of interest even into these framers yet leaving the focal area to maintain its prominence and natural function by possessing the lion's share of the overall impact.

Additional interest can be woven in, with a natural appearance, by not positioning groupings with the same number of pieces in them next to each other. This will appear both more natural and more esthetical by alternating groups of ones, threes, and fives. Thus a grouping of one should lie next to a grouping of three or five, a three next to a one or five, and a grouping of five next to a one or three. In more intricate designs, this is not always possible, but this looks quite pleasing.

Figure 6-25 Building interest through grouping

Perfect Design

Figure 6-26 Examples of achieving impact

Let's Design!

MORE VARIETY = LESS IMPACT

LESS VARIETY = MORE IMPACT

Chapter 7

Principles of Landscape Design

When designers reference the principles of landscape design, there probably comes to mind the idea of order and layout, often mixed in with ideas of balance and some kind of focal point. There is not much discussion of ratios, or exactly *how to* balance an area or *add or subtract* emphasis, how secondary axis lines might look, differences in frames and locations, the amount of variety per square foot, or designing by the individual function of each of the parts. Even the basic ingredients of these principles are not always in agreement within the vast array of landscape books. For example, is color a principle in the design process or a part of a later selection process?

Principles are in essence the guidelines of good compositional arrangement. The depth of understanding these principles—i.e., good arrangements—are more often found in the art books than in the landscape books for these teach the more in-depth fundamentals of proper visual construction to be presented and showcased to specific audiences.

Yes, there are site plans and contours, drainage considerations, and such; but a solid hold of these basic *principles of presentation* will anchor our vision, logic, and grip on individual skill sets of designing. I will present these as what I believe are the cornerstones of landscape design but with the caveat of placing these, as always, in a logical hierarchical format walking us through process in an organized way. Thus we will look at:

Purpose, Order, Balance, Harmony, and Interest.

1. Purpose

This is the ultimate reason anything in the world of landscaping exists—the focus, the visual implementation of what we wish to create, the driving force behind the process. This is the ability to take our vision and ***picture it complete.*** In other words, this is where we are going. This is what it will become. This is what it will say. It is the invisible hand of visual design, as in its economic counterpart, that keeps us committed to what we originally imagined. As we look down at that sheet of blank paper that will soon be covered with lines and circles and scribbles and erasures, it is there to remind us of why we design in the first place—to bring a concept to a living picture!

2. Order

This gives our purpose and theme a starting point, a beginning of structure, a basic underlying guide to arrangement, and a basic placement of functions within the entire arrangement. This is the vision we established in our bubble drawing that lays out the expectations of permanent features. This is making sure people easily flow through the area, that it makes sense to them, and where the interesting things might show up.

This is the check for adequate emphasis. "Is there enough space allotted?" This includes our check for angles. "Is the view from the kitchen window looking its best, straight on, and at a ninety-degree angle?" "Is there good pattern?" "Is the pathway leading to something significant? Where I would expect it to be?"

Order begins to build ***structural expectations*** into the design, those parts and functions that lie in areas where they naturally should be and without much surprise since it needs to be readily identifiable. It is creating the visual aesthetic center, the background or grouping creating closure, or the irregular triangle points made from the placement of three structural points. Order is the geometric framework built into the design. **Order gives structure a starting point!**

3. Balance

This is the softer side to the more rigid principle of order. As order brings alignment and agreement between the geometric parts (lines, points, space, shapes, and patterns), balance will direct the visual weight (or appearance of weight) between the sides of one or more axis lines. This in itself creates geometric interest, as will all of structure to a lesser degree. Balance then goes a bit further and contributes to the process by giving some additional and possibly unexpected aspects of interest through various left/right and top/bottom combinations of *weighting the composition*.

Taking this a bit further, as order is the expectations **throughout** the composition, balance is the arrangement **around** the center of the composition. We quickly sense an order to things for that is the way our minds were created. We try to find the order and balance in everything that we see. In a visual presentation or design, we also look for that centerpiece, the place that we could put our pointer finger under and just spin it around like a top if we had the strength.

So although these two principles are closely related, they are also one following the other. Order sets the expected visual stage, and balance is woven into those settings. They are distinct and separate pieces that together create a strong and unified framework. When we say that something is *perfectly balanced*, what we are actually saying in *designer-speak* is that there is perfect order, which includes equal symmetrical balance.

Substituting various visual weights then alters and softens this perfectly symmetrical view of order. It is this equation that reminds us that two regulating hands are involved in the equation **Structure = (Order + Balance)**. Order is established in the kingdom first; we then take a more balanced approach to rule over it!

4. Harmony

Unity and harmony are virtually synonymous with landscape designers using both terms quite interchangeably. I would surmise that there are actually two aspects of this unity/harmony circumspection running through our designs, especially as they become larger in scope. By separating the two, I see **unity** as it relates and gives oneness to the whole and entire picture, the essence of the total landscape. Good structure is the basis of good unity. I see **harmony** as the smaller thread that weaves itself through enough parts of the landscape to be well noticed, spotted here and there, and enough to remember that "I just saw that" but not so much to be everywhere. I like knowing that we must still be in the same book as we walk from chapter to chapter. This is based upon good recognizable structure into the design. Order and balance result from a number of elements in both position and repetition. Add specific elements to extend and broaden the harmony running through the design, and we will get unity!

Unity = (Structure + Harmony)

Even though these two terms are seemingly interchangeable, it is to the designer's advantage to make a clear distinction between the two. We might think of it as such: You may be one of a million sports fans that follow the Dallas Cowboys, all unified under one great cause. But without further interaction among all of you, there is no camaraderie, no support, no community, and no interaction. There is plenty of big-picture unity but no personal harmony.

Within a solid structure, harmony ensures that a number of elements, even smaller ones, repeat their visual nature, as all of nature does, to guide the eye throughout out the entire space. The cohesiveness that structure shouts out to us is also held together in the gentler rippling that we simply find flowing subtly in and out of the composition. You can think of it like this:

Unity = Oneness
Harmony = Cohesiveness

5. Interest

This is the part of the design process that comes alive in our landscapes, whether in the corner lot of suburbia or the commercial office building set deep in the downtown area of the city. Interest is set into our design, sometimes methodically and sometimes on more of a whim, as we are standing there at the garden center. It is the time we actually make a **selection** as to what things will be. Interest is built on variety, which includes designing different aspects, different looks, and different contrasts with different desires, all within a garden setting.

I will say that all too often this is where people start. They come in and fill a cart or two with just a general idea of where it is all going. Believe it or not, this is where many people begin. We spend many an hour with our bedside manners of design advice, gently asking or precipitously advising as to how an arrangement might be put together based upon what they have already selected.

Now not all landscaping is intended to create interest, as when we are using landscaping to hide something (no interest please!) or soften a look (foundation plantings). But when we truly desire interesting aspects, we gravitate to color, height, texture, and such with a decent amount of variety mixed in.

At this point, it seems appropriate to ask, "How much interest, or variety, can be put into a design without it becoming too busy?" This is a great question, however a bit illusive and not readily addressed in the landscape design books. **Too much variety** (and thus interest) can become very busy, a bit chaotic, even creating its own dissonance. We probably have all seen examples of landscapes that are overdone. Oh, but wait! **Too little variety** in the presentation slides into stoic, without movement for the eye, even boring. Where is the number, or range, that guides the amount of variety within a specific area?

If we trust our math and our aesthetical geometry, we should have confidence that there is a ratio out there somewhere in the great unknown that balances structure with interest. I will say that, for myself, it was by trial and error (much as with the ancient Egyptians

Principles of Landscape Design

and Babylonians) and by using the eye to try to discover the math and find an underlying ratio that made the design simply *look right*.

Now variety is not the same as the number of elements or plants. Variety is the sum total of how many **different types of looks** appear in the landscape area. If we have one hydrangea, three azaleas, five hosta, and seven coral bells, we have four varieties. It becomes a bit tricky if we have two different cultivars of hosta and three different cultivars of coral bells. As the designer, you will need to decide if therein lies enough contrast to count these as additional varieties. Variety also includes any other elements as art, boulders, benches, and so on. In this analysis, we have used the number range of 8 to 12 as the divisor of the area's square feet to yield an aesthetical number of variety to use:

$$\textbf{\textit{Amount of Variety within an area}} = \frac{ft^2}{(8 \text{ to } 12)}$$

As in the Fibonacci sequence, this tends to work better as the bed size increases. Thus a bed size of about ten to twelve square feet would result in just one variety. We remember though that this is not just one plant but one variety. This ratio is well satisfied by putting three small roses here or five medium hosta. This is still just one variety; and it's variety, not amount, that counts. Thus,

$$50 \; ft^2 \; bed = \frac{(5 * 10)}{(8 \text{ to } 12)} = \frac{50}{8 \text{ to } 12} = 4 \text{ to } 6 \; varieties$$

$$100 \; ft^2 \; bed = \frac{(10 * 10)}{(8 \text{ to } 12)} = \frac{100}{8 \text{ to } 12} = 8 \text{ to } 12 \; varieties$$

$$500 \; ft^2 \; bed = \frac{\left(12\frac{1}{2} * 40\right)}{(8 \text{ to } 12)} = \frac{500}{8 \text{ to } 12} = 42 \text{ to } 62 \; varieties$$

There is also quite a nice relationship between impact and interest, and it is easy to alter a design to increase or decrease either of them. By increasing the amount of variety, we lower the amount of impact. We can think of impact as a concentration of importance and relevance, and hence we whittle away at its primary job of commander in chief by increasing the notoriety and relevance of all the interesting details that surround it. If we wish to increase the impact of an area, we can just do the reverse and reduce the amount of interesting things competing with the focal area for attention. This includes the framers also; for at times, they are, or become, too large in proportion to the focal point and can even compete with it.

Impact is that general word we use to sum up all the attributes that make up its importance. It consists of size, color, and position. These three ingredients cover the actual mass we see **(size)** + the most notable feature of interest **(color)** + the proximity of elements **(position)**. Hotter colors are seen as stronger, almost coming forward at the viewer, and they are the easiest to quickly see. Therefore, a weak focal area may just need a good under planting of high color perennials versus replanting with larger shrubs to bring out its high position. Likewise, trimming the framers, or using cooler colors in those areas of interest, settles things down a bit in those particular spots. We can think of impact like this:

$$\textit{Impact = (Size + Color + Position)}$$

Chapter 8

Applying Mathematics and Geometry to Landscape Design Principles

As the designer, you will apply all the principles of landscape design, and you can pull any number of useful tools out of your toolbox as you arrange and rearrange the various visual relationships within the landscape. Proportion and balance are ratios. Borders and beds are lines and angles. Focal points and framers are inequalities. Unity and harmony equate to pattern and numerical repetition. Selection is a function of variety.

This will help us be more in tune with the lingo and the interconnections we traverse through as we will quickly take hold of what part of the plan we are addressing and exactly where we are in the planning process. We might think that we are being overly sensitive here, as when we discuss the parts or functions of our automobile. Tires are the things, but we could call them *car movers* (the function). However, we call the lights by function, we *turn on the lights* as if they were the things. The bulbs (what they are) are what we actually *turn on* so that they *light up* (the function). There is a profound difference when we fully comprehend the entire concept of design and understand the particular aspect it entails!

Each principle and each function within the landscape can be expressed in terms of mathematics or geometry, and in this section, we will look at those guiding concepts in that perspective. Here we will take a look at mathematical applications as they relate to a particular principle or function in the design process. We will look at the mathematical *truisms* of landscape design as each one of these is its own equation or inequality to guide the design from initial concept to final selection.

10 Mathematical Truisms of Landscape Design

1. Contents   > (Total Space x 80%)
2. Structure   = (Order + Balance)
3. Focal Area   = (Space – phi)
4. Focal Area   > (Left Frame + Right Frame)
5. Arrangement   > Selection
6. Impact   > (Interest + Variety)
7. What Things Do   > What Things Are
8. Elements   > One Function

9. Variety   = $\dfrac{Square\ Feet}{8\ to\ 12}$

10. Repetition   > All other attributes to create harmony.

Table-3. 10 Mathematical Truisms of Landscape Design

All of these truisms are each part of visual and, hence, landscape design. Each of these revolves around the **Universal Equation of all Visual and Landscape Design.** This basic formula is central to all visual design. And although it seems elementary, it is oft set aside as we add this and that to the design. This equation is, as easy as it seems, stated as such:

$$\textit{All Visual Design} = \\ (\textit{Left Frame} + \textit{Center Focal} + \textit{Right Frame})$$

1. Contents > (Total Space x 80%)

Looking at space as it relates to the broader area of intended use, we confine it and give it closure in one way or another. When we assign certain functions to certain elements, they take on certain jobs. However, when we do not allot enough space within the entire space for each element to do its proper job, the design suffers. This truism states that if the entire allotment of all the elements we will be using is not adequate, below a specific percent of the total area, they cannot do their intended function. There is simply not enough substance to work with to create the presentation effectively.

The most obvious situation is when the total amount of plant material (plus all the other elements) does not make the bed look *full*. It can look empty, thin, or even quite anemic. Quite often we see this when the main visual element in the bed is the mulch or the river rock. Whether intended or not, the bed looks out of sync. Something just doesn't look right. We don't get that warm feeling. There is simply not enough substance to work the visuals as needed.

Figure 8-1 Fuller beds just look better.

By trial and error, we have come to apply this **Rule of 1/5s** to create a minimum percent not to go below. In this, we allot four-fifth of the space (80%) to form and mass (elements including all our plant materials). The remaining one-fifth (20%) applies to what we call **flooring materials**—groundcovers or wood or rock mulch.

Perfect Design

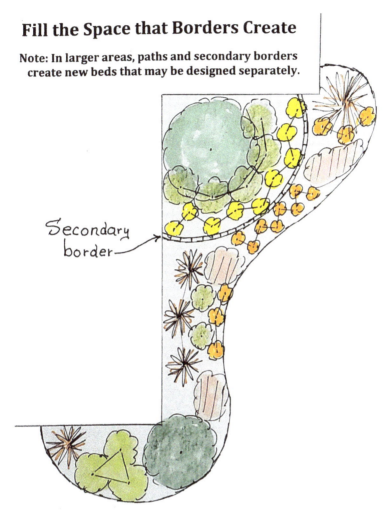

Figure 8-2 Filling the space that borders create

    This is the minimum ratio. However, for a richer, fuller, warmer, and very much more impactful presentation, the space can hold even near to 100 percent plant materials and other elements. Landscaped areas with this amount of material needs little or no mulch since the plants themselves, with their close proximities, are their own *living mulch*. The lower the ratio of space filled, the more the landscape bed will lose its impact. Regrettably, there are times when the wood or rock mulch has actually become the most prominent feature in the landscape and hence has become the unfortunate and unintended focal point!

In this light, we also violate the **Rule of Expectations**. We can compare this to a room in a house where we do not expect—for example, the living room—to be overflowing with pieces of furniture, tables, shelves, knickknacks, and such. We cannot since we must allow for pedestrian flow throughout, something very expected and accepted. However, we usually do not establish a planting bed for people to enter and walk through. We expect it to be somewhat full of plants. That is the reason it exists in the first place. At some point, the area begins to warm and come to life as we add plants, thus reducing the amount of *flooring* that we see. We can certainly use this 80/20 rule as a general guide in our landscape designs.

2. Structure = (Order + Balance)

We have given some discussion to this fundamental equation. Structure must come from somewhere, and if we do not quite know where it originates, it may become a bit shaky in our design. Both small to large landscapes need a framework, a must in every visually aesthetical arrangement. Just as we call the meeting to order and then set the general agenda before us, we set in order the supporting pieces of the landscape and then soften them up a bit where we can.

3. Focal Area = (Space – phi)

This is a point of discussion that raises its head in many a landscape design. We need to emphasize the focal area, but how do we determine what is enough to make a visual difference? Often this area is left undermanned in the design, not enough to overcome the activity surrounding it and comes out weak when it should be commanding the space.

Over the years, we have continually used 30 percent to 40 percent of the space to build and develop the impact a landscape needs. Much less than this percentage appears to come up short on presentation. It is here that the **Rule of 1/3s** works well, especially as the edges of the focal area begin to blend in with the other plantings. Often the focal area is not a perfect circle or ellipse, thus making it difficult to definitively decipher what the length across the bed actually is or the horizontal volume in the spot of emphasis.

Suffice it to say that by applying the underlying visual prowess of phi, we can land on a slightly better percentage, although in this application it might not be as critical as in other steps. As a calculation, we take 100 percent of the area, leave 61.8 percent (phi) for all the intermixing of the various functions and elements, but hold fast to the remaining 38.2 percent for our concentration of power. This is the percent we want to own as we put the show together!

4. Focal Area > (Left Frame + Right Frame)

This is such an easy mistake to make in a visual design. We can even apply our **Universal Rule of Design** (LF + Center Focal + RF) and still come up short because the proportions are incorrect. Just a walk or drive around the neighborhood will probably reveal a number of violations. We remember our plantings of three but set aside the functions of each. Anytime three or more plantings occur, unless set forth as a primary structure, background, a hiding feature, or a hedge, the center element focalizes while the outer two pieces frame. Remember:

Focal Points shout. Framers point!

5. Arrangement > Selection

Herein lies a tough act in convincing the average home landscaper that **where** they put something outweighs **what** they put there. In a world of aesthetical relationships, perspective, proportion, and percentages, the geometry definitely sets the stage before the actors are picked. Sadly, great selections do not overcome poor arrangements, even though good arrangements may overshadow some poor selections. Placement over pickings makes for a great performance!

6. Impact > (Interest + Variety)

When we choose to highlight a planting area, versus softening or hiding, our intent is to create impact or a stronger emphasis. This is why we prioritize this aspect. We create larger focal areas, make sure framers do not overshadow the focal area, and have everything sitting in a nice allocation of structure. We do not want interest to rule everything, only an active participant of the main event. We then, by design, gently guide the eye through the rest of the landscape. We first make the show big and exciting. After our guests arrive, they can enjoy its more interesting features.

7. What things do > What things are

The function of what an element does rules the day. This occurs, for example, when we need to hire an accountant. Who we hire is far less important than the position we hire. We need to fill the role, the function, or the position of an accountant. Whether Joe, Jill, Bob, or Alice does it is obviously less important than filling the vacancy. Later we can enjoy placing the ads, doing the interviews, and choosing the candidate (selection).

8. Elements > One Function

So often an element is bound to a single function in the design. But unless we allow for more than one function from a single element, we are stuck applying our Universal Equation by starting over and over again. By allowing, for example, the right frame of an area to become the left frame of an adjoining area or secondary framers to become subfocal points, we can continue to build a series of smaller (LF + Center Focal + RF) areas within the wholeness of the entire landscape.

This allows us to go around corners, fill the various smaller spaces created by a longer winding border, or use the framers from smaller portions of the landscape (as far left and far right) to also use as secondary framers for the larger composition. This flexibility will allow us to design flawlessly and without limitations quite large, intricate, and extensive landscape areas by simply connecting the framers of one smaller section to another no matter how irregular the beds or borders are.

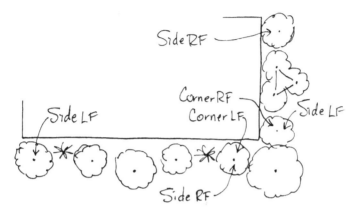

Figure 8-3 Example of elements having multiple functions

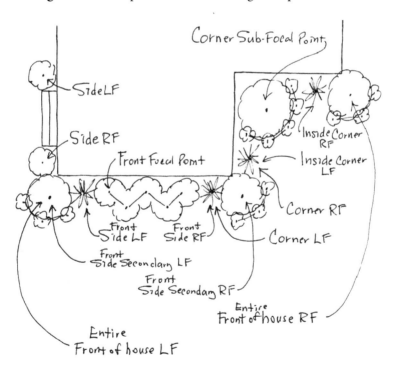

Figure 8-4 Example of elements serving more than one function

Applying Mathematics and Geometry to Landscape Design Principles

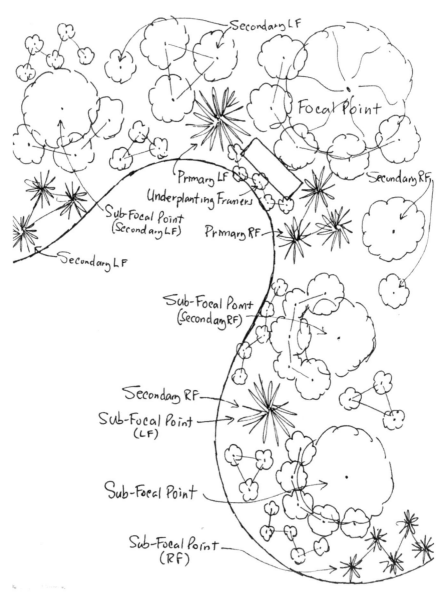

Figure 8-5 Example of larger landscape with elements serving more than one function

9. Variety $= \dfrac{\textit{Square Feet}}{8 \textit{ to } 12}$

There is a percent of our space that will naturally be ascribed to creating interest. Trial and error, our eyes, or years of experience will no doubt converge on that *just right* look. Our best calculations result from taking the square footage of the entire visual area and dividing that number by 8 to 12. This gives somewhere around a divisor of 10 on average depending on plant size (shrubs versus perennials etc.), plantable space available (allow for walks and such), and your own personality and desires of adding more or less variety and interest to your masterpiece!

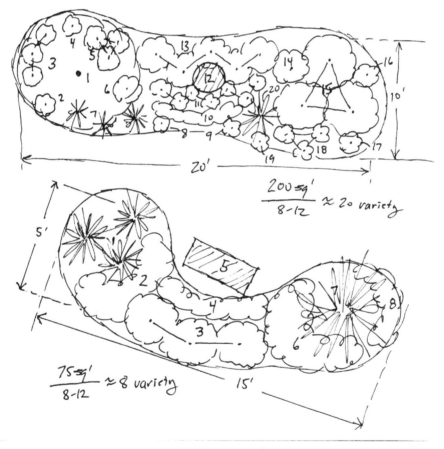

Figure 8-6 Examples of variety

Applying Mathematics and Geometry to Landscape Design Principles

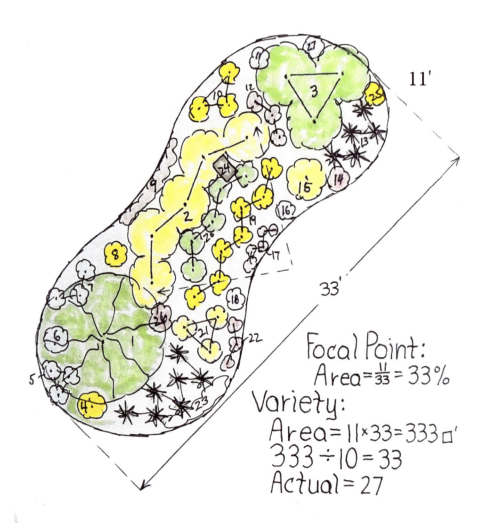

10. Repetition > All other Attributes to Create Unity and Harmony

As we cannot put all our marbles in one bag, neither can we entrust our *oneness of composition* to one element. No matter how large, colorful, or impactful something is, it is no match for numbers. Repetition is actually **twofold**. First it is telling us that something here will continue over there, thus persuading our eyes to move along throughout the landscape. Secondly, repetition is bringing a quiet comfort to us as we continue seeing old friends along the way. Yes, we see new things but in a company of nicely familiar furnishings.

Repetition leads to pattern. Pattern is what brings forth that aesthetical pleasure in the brain of seeing interrelated pieces and cognitively putting them together to discover the unity and harmony set before us. Our brains live for these moments!

All ten of these truisms support this universal equation: (LF + Center Focal + RF). This is incorporated in at the very beginning as we see an unfinished area in front of us. Our initial question will always relate to how this area can be visually anchored with a more central or naturally appearing middle and some concept of left and right forms on either side. As we first visualize a possible area to consider for a landscape or garden, we need to search for that middle ground in which to build that visual presentation. As we search for possible ways to frame the area, left and right sides may be anywhere from perfectly matched bookends of existing structures or plantings to simply a rough concept of possibilities that we can build upon as we design the area.

As human beings, we are wired to look for order and balance and hence good and logical layout and structure. We feel satisfied and content in and about such visually balanced areas. We tend not to even overly consider the surrounding order and balance when all is well. When it is not present, however, we immediately sense that the view in front of us feels a bit funny, it leans this way or that, turns us away, or gives us a chaotic sense about the design. Occasionally we are in a room where the walls have different colors, or the carpet has an extremely busy pattern, tables may not match exactly, the podium

Applying Mathematics and Geometry to Landscape Design Principles

is off centered, or doors and windows have been added for necessity and not for beauty. These things are immediately observed and can truly bristle at us.

Recently we were asked to design the front of a larger home. There were over twenty individual smaller sides which made up the front side of the house. Some were around bay windows. Some simply went in and out, and some around the front door area. Things can quickly become overwhelming. This is where it is essential to divide and conquer.

The door was somewhat centrally located with immediate left and right areas close enough to work with. Even though not perfectly matched in area and length of sides, we could make them appear more like framers by placing similar plantings and *weight* each side with a nice balance in mind. With some texturally matching shrubs, the sharpness of the smaller sides was diminished. We made sure there was brighter and more impactful plantings around the door and entranceway to pull the eye inward and not to the volume of shrubbery in the immediate left and right framer areas.

Following this, we then added similar evergreen plantings on the far left and right areas as secondary framers. Within each of these five areas (center focal, immediate left and immediate right framers, and secondary left and secondary right framers), we applied our Universal Formula (LF + Center Focal + RF). This appeared fairly obviously around the front entranceway and a bit looser in the framing areas. There were enough evergreens, similar plantings, and mulch to add harmony to the entire front, an area of nearly eighty feet across.

Figure 8-7 Harmonizing with grasses

Applying Mathematics and Geometry to Landscape Design Principles

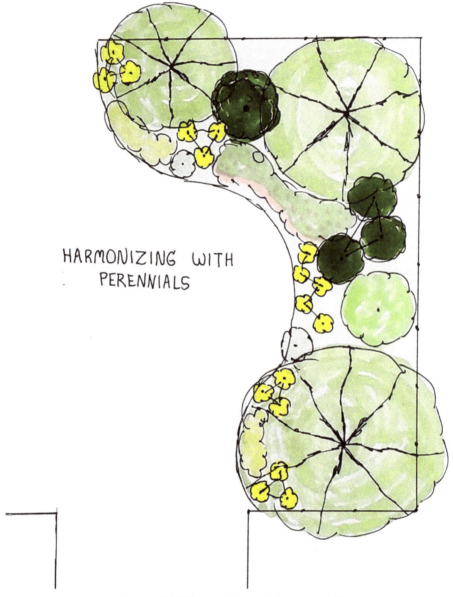

Figure 8-8 Harmonizing with perennials

Chapter 9

Specific Mathematical Applications to the Landscape

In this chapter, we will look at the principles of landscape design in a more purely mathematical sense. The ten mathematical truisms deliver a great analytical approach, especially for our more left-brain computational friends. Here we are going to take these principles, as well as other parts of the process, and apply specific formulas, ratios, numbers and placements as we dig deeper into the geometric aesthetics of landscape design and application.

1. Spatial Geometry

When we analyze spatial area, we are looking specifically at two aspects. First we look at the creation of the overall space, which includes both size and shape. Secondly, we are looking at the division of the space we just created. When considering the first objective, creating the overall space, we will initially be guided by three simple questions:

1. Where am I going to view this area from the most?
2. What is the overall purpose of, and appearance of, this space?
3. Is this generally more formal or informal?

As always, we try to simplify the process. Major mistakes can oft be avoided by answering simple questions. **To answer these**, go stand in the spots that you feel that you will view this from the most often. Tell yourself, or someone else, your intensions; and lastly, what does the rest of your yard, property, or neighborhood look like? It is best to match your intention with that of your entire view and to fit in well with your neighbors of whom you will be living nearby for hopefully the foreseeable future.

We can define these two concepts as:

> **Spatial Geometry**—Defines and describes the elements within a composition as purely visual objects (space, points, lines, circles, triangles, squares, ovals, polynomials, etc.) and the proximity and relationship between them

> **Aesthetical Spatial Geometry**—Observing or utilizing the traits, forms, characteristics, and distinctions of spatial geometry in visually pleasing arrangements

Formal areas lean toward straight lines, squares, rectangles, or circles, usually planted with close matching symmetry. Square beds will differ in total size, yet all sizes will imply expectations of matching features around a central element. Rectangles have an unlimited width to length ratio and come in many sizes too. A square lends itself to perfect symmetry as its borders have little option not to. Rectangles tend toward highly symmetrical plantings also; however, the ratio of width to length by itself can add to the aesthetics of the landscape area bed.

We have seen from long ago the application of this ***sweet spot*** in visual design, the golden segment of 61.8 percent of a line and its big brother, the golden rectangle, with the shorter side at 61.8 percent of the longer side. Thus the common sizes of 3 x 5, 6 x 10, 12 x 20, and so on form a very nice shape for our composition as these measurements are very close to the more perfectly aesthetical ratio of 61.8 percent seen in the golden segment and as the ratio of the shorter side to the longer side in the golden rectangle.

Since the early days of searching for perfect aesthetics, people have sought after a better understanding, a better way to obtain the optimal, almost divine, proportions and placement. Whether we begin with a mathematical foundation and build off of formula or allow our eye to get it right, we will all arrive at the same destination. Math confirms what our eye is telling us. The eye confirms what the math is dictating. Both are in agreement with each other.

Aesthetically, some rectangular shapes seem to be more pleasing to the eye than other shapes. Through experimentation, Gustav Fechner (1801–1887) did this in the late 1800s. He attempted, by example of various shapes and sizes of rectangles, to determine which shape would be the most pleasing to most people. Even though there were some mixed results, he concluded that the 3 x 5 proportional rectangle was generally the best aesthetical shape. It is quite a **simple little rectangle**. This ratio (3/5) is one of 60 percent. The short side is 60 percent of the long side. It is not much more than a square really. The 3 x 5 rectangle has exactly 67.7 percent (2/3) greater area than the 3 x 3 square, which is a somewhat pleasing ratio in itself as it equals 2/3 of a grid sectioned when applying the rule of 1/3.

As we look at the informal side of shapes, as the ellipse, this proportion seems to work just as well:

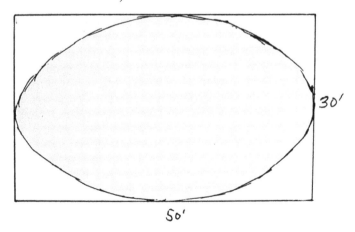

Figure 9-1 Informal shape of the ellipse

As does the famous peanut shape:

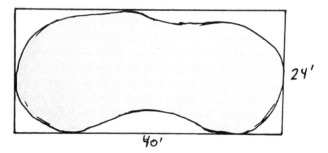

Figure 9-2 Informal shape of a *peanut*

That perfect, yet illusive, ***just-right-spot*** can be applied to an overwhelming basket of possibilities. Anything with an aesthetic posture, from a single point on a line (imaginary or not) to an area designated within a broader space and to focal points within the painting or the proportions of the makeup of man himself, can be described along the lines of this ratio.

And although seen in geometric shapes as in the pentagon and its triangular formations, the confirmation of the aesthetics was revealed in a wonderful and imaginative sequence of numbers. It was the well-respected mathematician named **Fibonacci** (1170–1240) who was credited with establishing this unique sequence (thusly called the Fibonacci Sequence). It is an amazingly simple sequence of adding two numbers together, starting with 1, and then adding the sum of the two numbers to get the next number in the sequence. So it looks like this:

$$1,1,2,3,5,8,13,21,34,55,89,144,233,377,610...$$
Equation 1. The Fibonacci Sequence

The ratio between consecutive numbers at first is rather general, but it quickly converges to the first number of any two numbers in consecutive order being 61.8 percent of the following number in the sequence. Conversely, and very uniquely, the second of any two consecutive numbers divided by the first number is equal to 1.618. The first number is 0.618 (61.8%) of the second. The second number is 1.618 (161.8% of the first). Thus:

$$\frac{377}{610} = 0.61803 \qquad \frac{610}{377} = 1.61803$$

$$377 \times (1.61803) = 610 \qquad 610 \times (0.61803) = 377$$

$$100\% - 61.803\% = 38.197\%$$

Equation 2. Computing the *golden segment*

This special distance and proportion, matchless of any other, seems to be distinctively human to ponder, enjoy, and excite. This spot on the line, that *oh-so-perfect placement* called the golden segment, is as much mathematical as it is aesthetical, as it divides the line into these two proportions. A 10' line divides at the 6.1803' (or 3.8197') mark. It provides a relationship between the two parts in that it divides the line or space at that particular position that the larger segment is exactly 1.61803 times the smaller section. It also provides an aesthetical spot of placement when we do not wish to use the mathematical middle of an area because it just seems to be very unnatural or fake. It is the default spot to help us make a solid second choice of locating the impact spot in the composition.

We can locate a tree in the back yard by applying this segment as such:

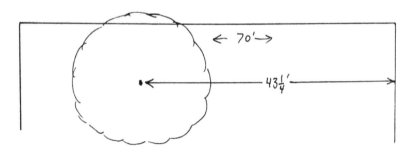

Figure 9-3 Tree placement with the golden ratio

In front or the side of the house, we might locate a tall shrub like this:

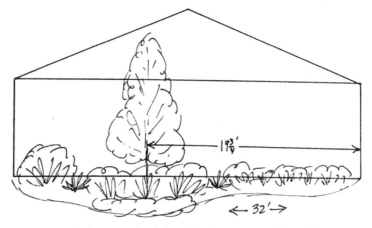

Figure 9-4 Placing a shrub beside a house using the golden ratio

We can also use this ratio to place a single element in any visually enclosed space by measuring out the golden section along one of the sides, mark the spot, and then place the item into the composition with its midpoint at that location.

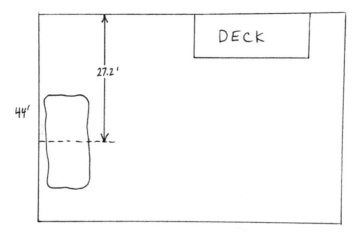

Figure 9-5 Pond placement in yard using the golden ratio

We can use this concept when creating a space inside of a space, as a smaller landscape bed within a larger bed.

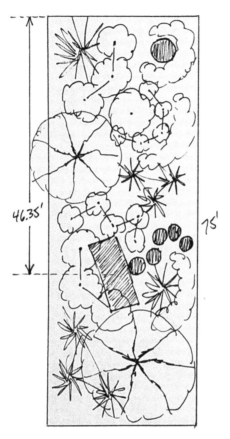

Figure 9-6 Bench placement in landscape bed using the golden ratio

Specific Mathematical Applications to the Landscape

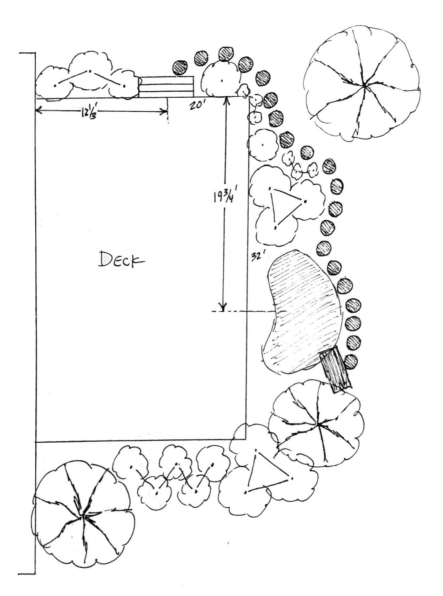

Figure 9-7 Using the golden ratio to position a pond beside a large deck. In addition, the golden ratio is used to align the steps.

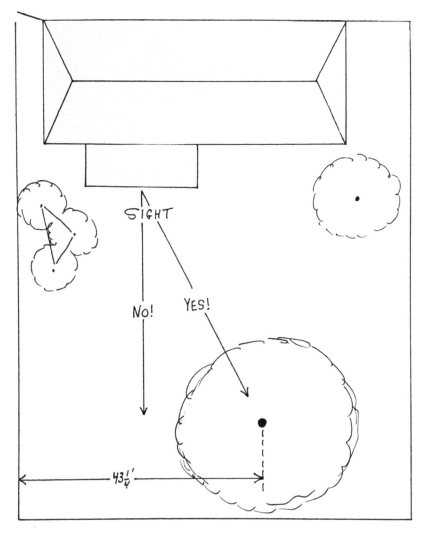

Figure 9-8 The golden ratio used for tree placement

This is undoubtedly why the **Rule of 1/3s** is so popular. It comes oh so close at 33.333 percent and 66.666 percent. From a grid perspective, using the **Rule of 1/5s**, we see divisions at 40 percent and 60 percent. Close approximations do give comfort, although both of these are just not quite there. We see a more rigid relationship in both of these spacing. When using the first ratio, 1/3 is actually half of 2/3, which is a bit formal and expected. The second ratio results in five equally spaced sections with placement at the 40 percent mark, which is exactly 2/3 of the larger 60 percent section. Not a terrible relationship but again very expected and not very exciting. Approximations are useful and get us close to that *sweet spot*. Fibonacci slides us over just a little bit.

2. Angles

Angles can be quite challenging to incorporate into a design. They seem to look good and they are simply necessary to use. They can look quite pleasing, sometimes not so much. The golden triangle, seen as the dissecting angles of a pentagon, is a triangle with angles of 36 degrees, 72 degrees, and 72 degrees and appears like this:

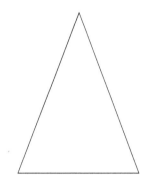

Figure 9-9 The golden triangle

These shapes may not be extremely pleasing in a landscape since we tend to acclimate to the more gentle shapes in horticulture, as a horizon, but may be more applicable in the vertical as trees and shrubs.

The angles that we will look at can relate to landscape size but mostly shape. Familiar angles are 360 degrees (circle), 180 degrees (line), 137.5 degrees (golden angle), 90 degrees (right angle), 45 degrees (half the right angle), and 42.5 degrees (180 degrees − 137.5 degrees). Lines and circles are very familiar, and we use parts of them continually in designs: a short connecting line here or a portion of the circle, the arc, there and so forth. I would strongly say that designers can sense that these angles *look right*, and therefore they are right. Your eye has done you well!

The numbers are intriguing also! The golden angle results from 360/phi = 222.5 degrees. The 360 degrees (circle) − 222.5 degrees = 137.5 degrees (golden angle). This is also an approximation of 90 degrees (right angle) + 45 degrees (1/2 right angle), which is = 135 degrees. This is close enough to use but the true better angle is there for us too.

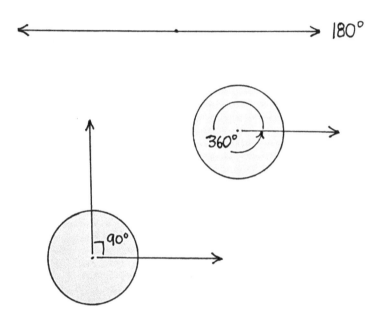

Figure 9-10 Angles and circles

Specific Mathematical Applications to the Landscape

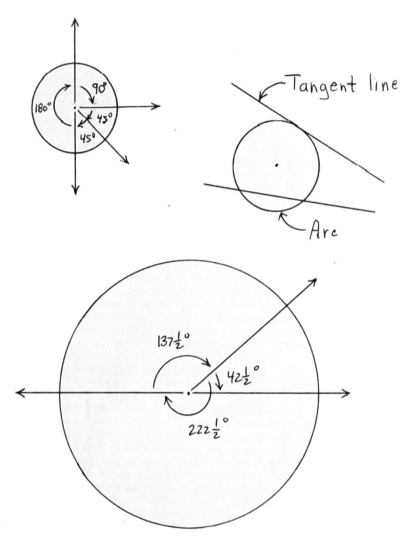

Figure 9-11 The golden ratio revealed in circles

Perfect Design

The angles of the golden triangle (36 degrees and 72 degrees) are acute, a bit sharp for informal application, but applicable for a bit of interest or a vertical statement.

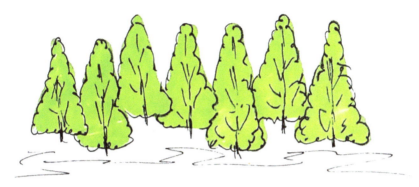

Figure 9-12 Using a golden triangle to place trees

Right angles (90 degrees) are built upon a fortress, expected to be strong, with one right angle leading to the next right angle, to the next corner, or the next box. This is excellent use in establishing a formal presentation and can be used both vertically (buildings, fences, posts, trellises) and horizontally (beds, walks, borders, edges).

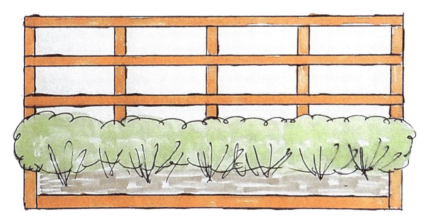

Figure 9-13 Example of right angles providing structure

Specific Mathematical Applications to the Landscape

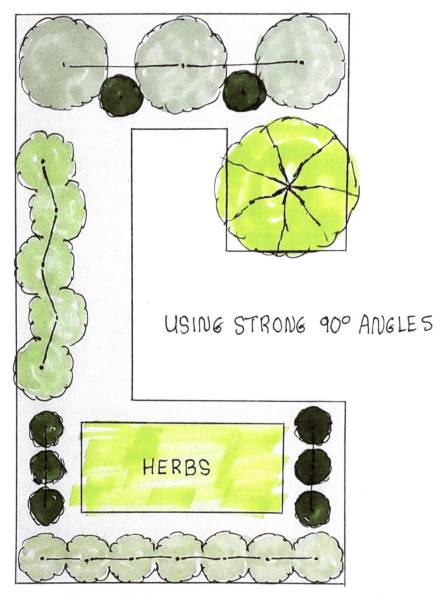

Figure 9-14 Using strong 90-degree angles in garden bed

Angles of 45 degrees (half of 90 degrees) are the equivalent of 1/4 spatial area of a line or bed. It is fairly predictable and stoic,

Perfect Design

utilized in more formal settings with predictable placement and elements.

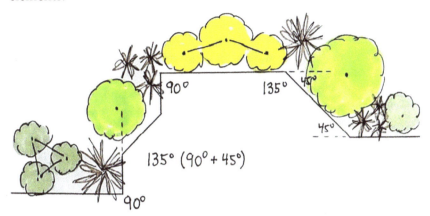

Figure 9-15 Using 45-degree angles with 90-degree angles along a wall

On the softer side, we see pleasing angles at 222.5 degrees (360 degrees × phi (.618)), 137.5 degrees (360 degrees − 222.5 degrees), and 42.5 degrees (222.5 degrees − 180 degrees), all of which seem to rub us just kind of right. In a circle of 360 degrees, they appear as:

Figure 9-16 The golden angle in a round bed

Interestingly enough we see that phi of phi of 360 degrees = 137.5 degree!

Specific Mathematical Applications to the Landscape

We see these angles continually used in landscape borders with the curves (arcs), fence enclosures, or anytime we use three elements to form a triangular pattern somewhere in the landscape. Although challenging to measure, the flowing curves of a border emulate continual angles in the ebbs and flows of these curves:

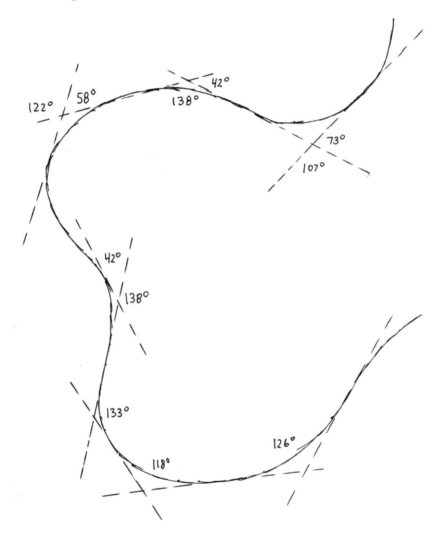

Figure 9-17 Estimating angles of curves

Perfect Design

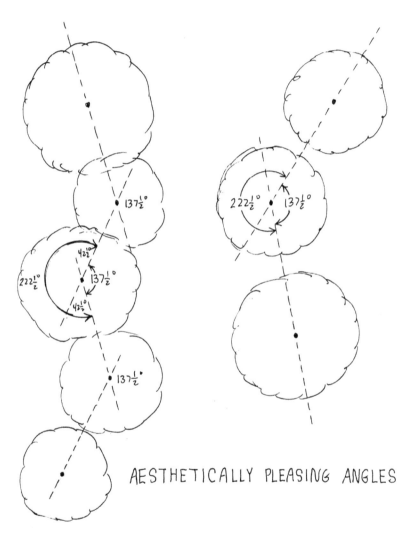

Figure 9-18 Aesthetically pleasing angles

Specific Mathematical Applications to the Landscape

Meandering borders create both **pockets** (flared out toward the viewer) and **divots** (flared in). We hold valuable things in our pockets; things of lesser value are relegated to the divots. Angles that hover around the pleasing angle of 137.5 degrees are leading the eye to the next pocket of valuable space:

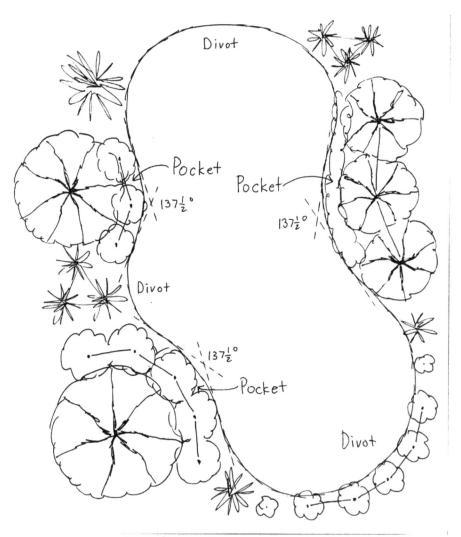

Figure 9-19 Using the golden ratio to create pockets

Acute angles of less than 90 degrees tend to turn the eye sharply indicating a change in direction, pattern, or a ceasing of additional material ahead. When we see angles that are acute, we sense the space closing in on us, or ending, versus the openness of the abstruse angle (greater than 90 degrees). I call these angles at or less than 90 degrees **visually sharp**, somewhat uncomfortable in today's more informal landscapes unless used as a small point of interest.

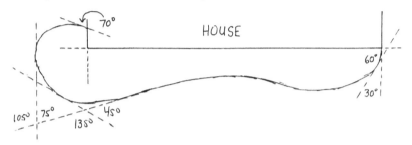

Figure 9-20 Creating *softer* angles using the golden angle

Angles closer to our more comfortable 137.5 degrees are **visually softer.** This is such a common observation that when we say to a homeowner that they might soften up the borders, they know exactly what is meant: to increase the angles of the ebbs and flows to move the eye more gently across the horizontal parts of the landscape presentation.

I recall recently placing a rustic fence around our Idea's Garden here at the garden center. We placed several six-, eight-, and ten-foot fence pieces on the ground around the end of the garden, moving here and adjusting there until it too had that just right feeling. This was by eye, with the definite intent of making this area look nicely softer. Later I put the protractor on some of the angles just to test the eye, and yes, they were as close to the golden angle as the eye alone could do!

One year, we spent several days resetting about 100' of fences around a number of areas in our display gardens. We were intent on changing the look, the feeling of closure, and making the gardens more separate from the parking and general areas. Nearly all the effort went into finding the correct angles of the fence pieces in order to obtain the correct feeling. I still am quite amazed at the power and significance of creating that perfect angle within the design.

3. Geometry of Structure

At this point, we can observe how angles dictate the size, shape, and movement around the space that we created. The next natural step would be to build the structure (order + balance) within that space. We can do that with virtually any number of elements; however, elements greater than about five, unless a hedge or a foundation planting, begin to look a bit overloaded for the job they are doing. They can become scattered throughout without distinct pattern. Consequentially, they are just loosely growing plantings if not given a good orderly alignment.

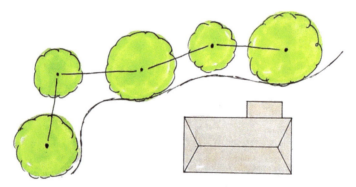

Figure 9-21 Creating structure with geometry

A single object of sizeable or noticeable mass, although with the appearance of structure, will also be seen as the focal point. This is the power and strength of a single piece. It stands alone, and because it is just one, it will be seen as something *expected* to stand alone. This is why weak focal points (inadequate size, color, or position) make weak landscapes. Each piece of the design needs to step up and fulfill its given role!

Perfect Design

Figure 9-22 Building structure with single objects

The most exciting aspect of coordinating and positioning structural points within the space is by utilizing the number three. Any time that three of *something* is used, it will form a **visual triangle**. And that visual triangle can take on any number of angles, sizes, or proportions. We are usually not looking for our *structural threesome* to look man-made, unless we are implementing a more formal presentation. We do have, however, regular triangles, golden triangles, acute or abstruse triangles, informal triangles, and perfect triangles in our toolbox.

Is there a way to more aesthetically position all three points of this triangle, which will then show the position of the three structural pieces? I am convinced of the aesthetical power of the triangle in all visual presentations including the landscape presentation, and let's see how we can apply some geometry here to find these three positions.

Let us begin with the **Fibonacci sequence** where the ratio between any two consecutive numbers in that sequence is the same. For these consecutive numbers, the first divided by the second will equal about 0.618, or in other words the first number is 61.8 percent of the second number. This is that golden section, that aesthetically pleasing point on a line that for some mysterious reason resonates with our artsy spatial makeup. But what if we incorporate this golden section on the three sides that visually contain our landscape space? This would include the left, back, and right sides.

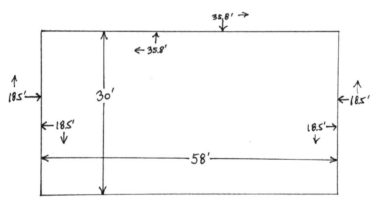

Figure 9-23 The golden sections in a landscape

Perfect Design

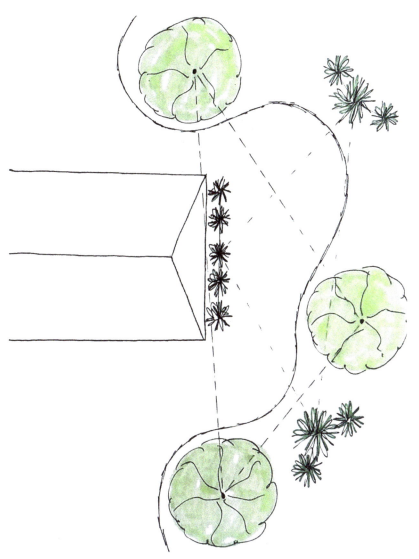

Figure 9-24 Building structure with triangles

Specific Mathematical Applications to the Landscape

Figure 9-25 Building structure with triangles

Perfect Design

By marking these three points at 61.8 percent on the outline borders, or the imaginary but implied containing line of the entire area, and then connecting these three points, we have in essence created a **Fibonacci Triangle**! This is *not* the Pascal triangle where the arrangement of the numbers within the triangle reveal the Fibonacci sequence. This is a visual relationship of golden section points that when connected create the **beautiful outlines of the Fibonacci sequence in triangular form**!

In other words, we are rotating the golden sections from one side to the next to the next to create the points of the angles outlining the Fibonacci triangle. We simply connect the points:

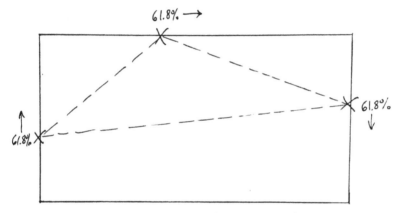

Figure 9-26 Using the points on the Fibonacci triangle to create structure

Specific Mathematical Applications to the Landscape

This process will locate the three points on the containment lines (whether seen or implied). And since we do not usually plant or position elements directly on these lines, they simply mark the location on each particular side. At this point, we position the pieces **into the composition**, at that mark, to show the midpoint of whatever structural piece we choose to use.

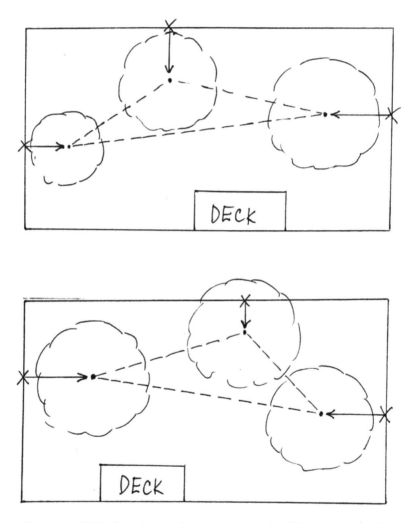

Figure 9-27 Deck and tree placement using the Fibonacci triangle

The Fibonacci triangle works so well that this can be applied to a gamut of various design decisions:

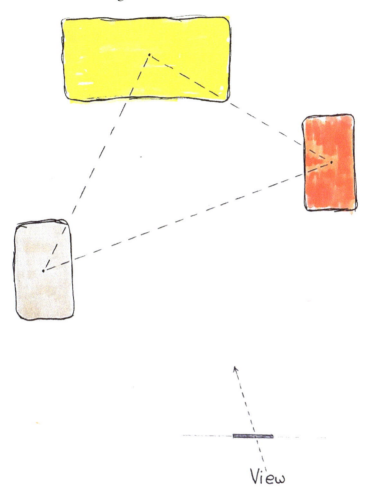

Figure 9-28 The Fibonacci triangle used to place three elements

Specific Mathematical Applications to the Landscape

There are going to be other things in these settings, such as other plants, chairs, tables, and so on; but these are the structural positions that we are locating more exactly which then allows for more freedom of placement of all those other things. Remember:

The easier it is to identify the structure and the purpose, the more freedom we have to add variety and interest.

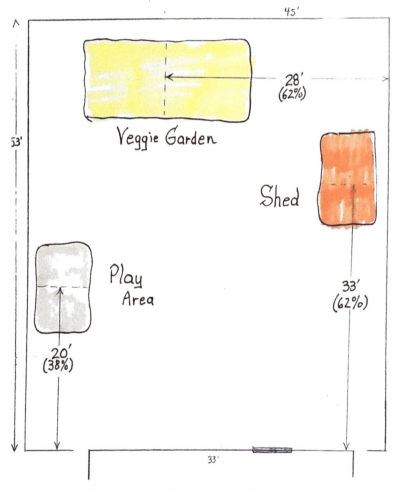

Figure 9-29 Backyard layout using Fibonacci segments

Perfect Design

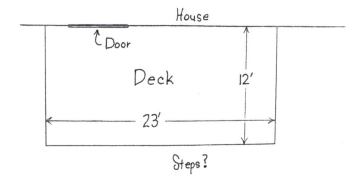

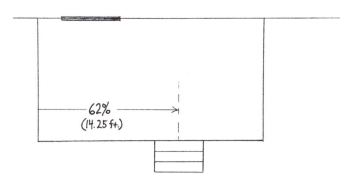

Figure 9-30 Using Fibonacci segment to place steps on desk

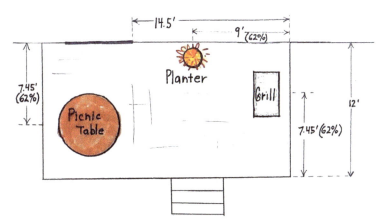

Figure 9-31 A potential porch layout using Fibonacci segments for placement

Now the question arises as "How deep into the composition?" For a single object, we can actually use the golden rectangle as a guide as to where this would be placed within the entire area. This gives us a *go-to-spot* that will yield an aesthetic position, even though there may be a number of other conditions to consider, such as blocking a view of the neighbor's garage or not blocking the view of the lake, etc.

This is a very workable process, based upon a proven ratio, within a visually contained space. However, a second consideration must be made. Once one of the elements is set in place (if large enough), the remaining visual length of one side may actually be reduced. We must account for that. We are looking for a visual answer where the initial placement can affect further positioning. Since something now *occupies* some of the visual space, we must now alter the remaining space for the other elements. In this example, we need to recalculate our new golden section from the portion of the side that we can now see. The math only makes sense applied this way since it is ultimately based on the visual area we actually perceive.

4. Focal Point Positioning

Here we will begin with the eye before we get to the numbers. We would be hard-pressed to say that the garden/landscape area does not have a *natural focal point*. There are areas that do not lend themselves to an area of high impact or a centered piece of interest, such as a foundation planting of just boxwoods, or the veggie garden, or that row of annuals along the driveway. But any garden bed large enough to be called a landscape will have some point of natural emphasis in one of these five geometric positions:

1. **The Natural Focal Point**—what appears to be visually centered
2. **The Middle Point**—the actual linier center
3. **The Highest Point**—elevated a bit above the rest
4. **The Pocket Point**—within the meandering border
5. **The Background Point**—in the middle of the large and obvious background piece

This is imperative in establishing order and balance in the arrangement. My first choice is always to select the more natural focal point area. It is difficult to fight against this spot, as we might be forever trying to ignore what is just too obvious. If we, for example, wish to locate the center of our planting area in the true middle of the house, despite that very large off-centered picture window to the right, it will always be there. The only way to move the eye from another object, as the window or the framers etc., is to do what we have previously discussed: we need to increase the impact of the focal point, and/or we need to decrease the impact of the other object(s).

We do this in different ways. First we can enlarge the plantings, add color, or add other pieces of interest to pull the eye back to the focal area. Secondly, we can reduce the impact, in this case of the large window, by covering it with larger noncolorful shrubs or possibly painting the frame a darker color (anything but white!) to lessen the impact. There is often more than one way to get where we want to go!

As the designer, we often work around existing objects. Because we are well aware of the **language of functions**, we can identify what the function of each existing element is. We can **change the function** by rearranging the existing elements or by adding other new elements.

We were recently challenged when we redesigned a very intricate, and somewhat confusing, landscape in front of a large-sized home. There were several shrubs that immediately seemed out of place and for good reason. Although nice, they were in positions that were very unsettling with little impact points or logical framing. The landscape area was full; however, it was not warm and inviting. Once we determined a good (LF—Center Focal—RF) structure, we changed a number of functions by removing, moving, and adding a variety of other pieces. Before we really got to add any more interest and color, it had already taken shape in and by itself by visually and orderly identifying these pieces and making sure they were doing what they should be doing! We can use these general guidelines in locating the center focal area of impact also.

Specific Mathematical Applications to the Landscape

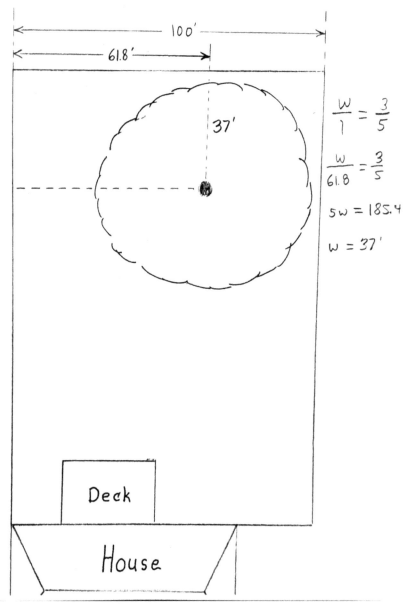

Figure 9-32 Single-tree placement with golden ratio

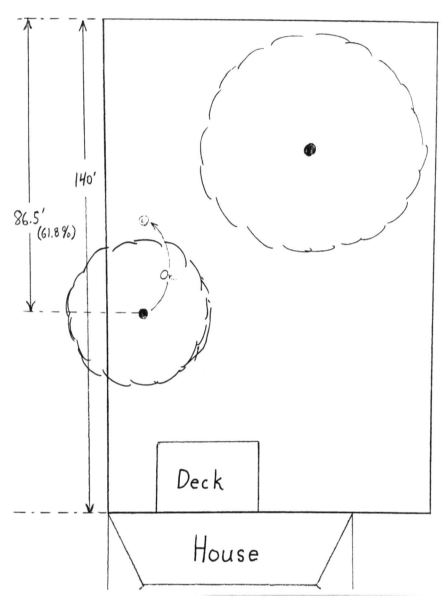

Figure 9-33 Two-tree placement using the golden ratio

Specific Mathematical Applications to the Landscape

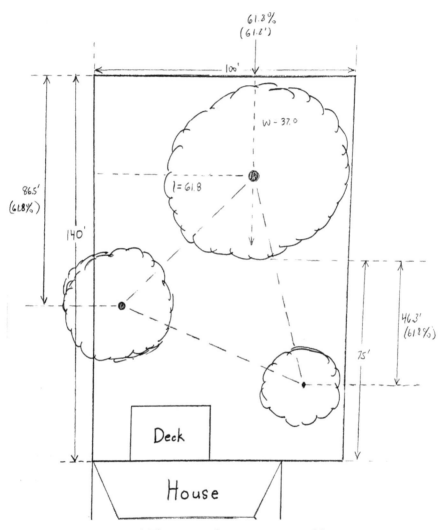

Figure 9-34 Three-tree placement using golden ratio

5. Framers

These are the two very obvious left and right, and possibly in front of, elements that tell the eye to "look here." They are pointing to something more impactful than everything else nearby. They are somewhat structural because they should contain nothing that brings more impact to them than to the focal area. Their job is simply to surround and point. They can be two elements or two groupings that provide roughly the same visual weight to either side.

Framers can be immediate (primary), positioned visually *just out of reach* of the focal point, or quite a distance away (secondary framers) as long as they appear to somewhat match and to lie somewhere within reasonable sight of each other. Those smaller plantings which lie directly in front of the focal point may be rightly called under framers if somewhat non-impactful or seen as part of the focal area if bolder or brighter in color as to attract the eye. There are those focal points that need no one to point them out. They are big, bold, and handsome. Use them when needed. In the geometric sense, framers are less impactful than the focal area next to it. Impact can be seen and defined as this:

Impact = (Size + Color + Position) > Remainder of Area

One feature alone may not be enough to pull the eye toward itself, and thus discretion lies with the designer as to how much, and in what combination of attributes, constitutes enough impact.

6. Harmony

This is repetition throughout the entire landscape area. Repetition creates visual movement that pulls the entire presentation together. This is what we call the power of unity; and it is seen more in the structure, focal area, and immediate framers.

We also see a different kind of unity: the more subtle pieces running through here and there, symmetrical or sometimes not, which are more passively placed just so we get a sense of gentle cohesiveness.

We may prominently plant a nice display of roses and then add just a single rose on each side to extend out the color and pattern. We then weave darker-leafed coral bells scattered in small groupings of three to add that bit of harmony, maybe even just popping up in a single planting here and there, not knowing exactly where one might just show up. Nonetheless, they are still doing their job of holding things together even at somewhat lower levels of recognition.

Likewise, we may decide on a nice hydrangea grouping at center stage with a rock wall in back for containment. In front lies a number of larger blue and green hosta and pulmonaria with intermixing colors. We then decide to use the variegation of other specific plantings to add some harmony. We plant smaller variegated hosta, liriope, and sedge using the creamy green and white stripes as a repeating (although not a perfectly matching) pattern. A *sprinkling* of smaller color and texture often injects **just enough to soften** the bigger picture and add **another layer of interest.**

Suffice it to say that this falls under the umbrella of variety. We need to take this into consideration when calculating how much overall variety goes into a design.

We would be looking to add these harmonizers with other bits of variety and interest keeping the amount within the safe zone in our computation:

$$Variety = \frac{Total\ Square\ Footage}{8\ to\ 12}$$

7. Interest

Here is the point where so many of us want to be. Finally! Oh, the colors! The sizes! The textures! This is what we live for and should! This is truly the topping on the cake. And like any good analogy, there should be more cake than topping. If we get too much, "Oh, my eyes!" If too little, "On our viewers go!" Since we discussed this earlier, let us just add these dimensional guidelines in our search for great interest in the right proportion. We find interest in these three ways:

1. A bit in its structure by its position, height, weight, and color. Also in the borders through their angles and meanderings.
2. Plenty in the focal point/area. Not because of its position, which is to be expected, but because of our intent to make it impactful. Here we use plenty of size, color, and texture.
3. A bit again in the somewhat unexpected places—the sub-focal areas, pieces of garden art, nicely textured filler plants, the small hanging basket hung on one of the trees, or the harmony we find in the perennials that we meet along our walks.

Now we need to see everything on **one big scale**. We must account for the shifting of impact as we add or subtract variety (and hence interest). **Impact and variety** are closely related: as we add variety, we lower impact. We are simply diluting the available resources to highlight our presentation. As we lower the amount of variety, we increase impact. We do indeed credit the math with setting us straight in so many areas, but I also give due credit to the trained eye of the designer who can judge well the things that go nicely into the composition and those things that ought not to be there!

These mathematical guidelines already establish a bit of interest in the composition through placement, although selection is still the real deal of being able to actually choose all those neat things to fill all those empty spaces in the design. It is what we do when we visit a garden center. It is the ultimate treat for the weekend warrior to fill a cart full of color and head home with a mission in their souls!

Chapter 10

Numbers Matter

Design reveals a sense of order and logic; and the use of certain numbers of an object, feature, or plant can add greatly to the outcome you are hoping to achieve. The design will be more logical and powerful when using numbers correctly, such as the following:

ONE—Shows power and authority. The ability to stand on its own.
TWO—Shows framing and balance. An awkward number if it's not doing its job.
THREE—The most natural of numbers. The ability to have a very pleasing effect on small groupings to bring informality to a planting area or to make a *grouping* become more noticeable when one just won't do. It is nature's nearly perfect number.
FOUR—Too many for framing since it will leave two on each side and is unnatural for groupings leaving an *air pocket* in the middle when planted in a row. Four can best be used in the background with three of *something* planted in the spaces between forming a group of seven.
FIVE—Forms a nice grouping in a focal area, a small hedge, a foundation planting, a background to a small bed, or adding structure to an area.
SIX—Can be as awkward as four, unless squeezed together to mask the actual number, thus forming one larger grouping.
SEVEN—Begins to form a hedge or larger grouping, depending on the size and shape of the bed.

Chapter 11

The Tools of Landscape Design

As the landscape area becomes larger, the design elements take on a more significant level of importance. The following pages will explore some of these spatial design concepts and tools in a more detailed aspect:

1. **Lines**
2. **Colors**
3. **Texture**
4. **Form and Shape**
5. **Numbers**
6. **Order**
7. **Balance**

1. Lines *are edges that pull your eye.*

   A. Think of lines as an outline of an inner shape
   B. Guides the eye, pulls the viewer
   C. Defines space (borders)
   D. Differentiates viewing area and planting area (grass area/mulched area)
   E. Differentiates public and private areas (sidewalk, fence, trellis)
   F. Horizontal lines spreads the eye, vertical lines lifts the eye

The Tools of Landscape Design

2. Color *plays with your emotions.*

    A. Seen as hot (red, yellow, orange), neutral (brown, black, grey), or cool (blue, green, purple)
    B. Hotter colors jump out at the viewer, cooler colors tend to recede
    C. Hotter colors tend to excite, cooler colors tend to calm
    D. Contrasting hotter and cooler colors next to each other will accent each other
    E. Burgundy and silver/gray can be good filler colors (coral bells, artemesia)
    F. White is usually used as a hot or highlighting color (as in a white picket fence and unfortunately the large garage door)
    G. Any striking color or variegated plant or object can be used in repetition to create harmony (liriope, hosta, coleus)

3. Texture *makes it appear as though you were touching it.*

    A. Usually lasts longer than color
    B. Gains more prominence up close
    C. Coarse and fine textures usually make a nice contrast (euonymus and ferns)
    D. Coarser plants (especially cooler colors) can add depth at the back of the bed
    E. Finer textures suggest a more formal, elegant feeling

4. Form *gives shape with depth.*

    A. Defined by their outline
    B. Holds their positions in the bed
    C. Similarly shaped plants, although different in variety, usually blend together well

5. Numbers *mathematically affect us.*

   A. Odd numbers (1, 3, 5) appear more natural and less formal
   B. Even numbers (2) frame a plant/object or (4) will fill in behind a set of 3 thus making a grouping of 7
   C. Gives a consistent message to the viewer

6. Order *establishes the rules.*

   A. Beginning of structure
   B. Sets boundaries and limits
   C. Creates stability and comfort in the layout

7. Balance *places the axis line(s).*

   A. Depends on the placement of *visual weights* within the area
   B. Larger, bolder, hotter plants/objects carry more visual weight than smaller, cooler ones
   C. Types of balance results from where the axis line(s) is placed

Formal Arrangement	*Informal Arrangement*
Match *identity* on each side	Match *weight* on each side
More expectation to see	More surprises to see
More even numbers are used	More odd numbers are used

Chapter 12

Ten Steps to a Great Landscape Design!

Quick Notes

This is the guide that we have used here at the garden center for many years as it provides a great overview of the process all at once. It is telling you the designer, in a somewhat condensed version, what we have been expanding on in this entire book. If you want a quick reference, or wish to share this with your designing friends, this makes a handy guide.

Ten Steps to a Great Landscape Design!

Vision/Theme

1. **Determine** the purpose and function of the various areas of the landscape.
2. **Envision** the entire landscape and its parts, as it will look when completed.

Arrangement

3. **Lay out borders**. (Create *Space*):
   a. Straight lines suggest a more formal setting; curved lines suggest less formality, with more rhythm and movement.
   b. Plants should *fit* proportionally to the size of the planting bed.

4. **Select a focal point(s)**. (Create *Impact*):
   a. Emphasize bigger, bolder, longer-blooming, and unique features.
   b. Think impact first, variety second.

5. **Add order and balance**. (Create *Stability*):
   a. Frame the focal point for added emphasis.
   b. Arrange similar *visual weight* throughout the entire area.

6. **Add harmony**:
   a. Select the same or similar plantings throughout the area (especially in larger beds).
   b. Repetition supports the theme and adds movement to the beds and borders.

Selection

7. **Generate interest.**
   a. Consider size, shape, color, texture, movement, appearance, and sound.

8. **Use contrast.**
   a. Structural plants (larger, bolder, more prominent) add impact when surrounded by smaller, less noticeable, or filler plants.

b. Hotter (brighter) colors next to cooler (darker) colors will tend to intensify and highlight each other. Hot colors *jump out*; cooler colors *recede*.
   c. Alternate groupings of 1s, 3s, and 5s (especially in larger beds).

9. **Start BIG, end small.**
   a. Begin with considering the larger purpose of creating the landscape, where larger items will be positioned, and finally what details and plant varieties to include in the design.
   b. Taller plants should tend toward the back, shorter in front (especially in deeper beds).

10. **Numbers matter.**
    a. Odd numbers (1,3,5) appear more natural and less formal.
    b. Even numbers (2) frame a plant/object and (4) *fill in* between odd become a more tightly planted visual *grouping*.
    c. Medium-sized groupings (5 to 7) form nice backgrounds or foundation plantings.
    d. Use ratios as guidelines in larger or more detailed plantings.
    e. Sketch out your design before you plant!
    f. Position everything in place before you plant—tweak now!
    g. Use proven planting techniques and water regularly.

This book has been written to specifically look at any visual design in a new and challenging way. We are looking to deepen our creative toolbox and strengthen our design ingenuity. We are expanding our knowledge, wisdom, and application of fundamental mathematical and geometrical guidelines to create new and exciting landscape designs for ourselves or our clients. We think differently, comprehend differently, process differently, and thus design differently!

As designers, or those becoming designers, we see the world as individual pieces working together based upon order, balance and purpose that bring forth merit, value, usefulness, and beauty. We sense the visual design principles incorporated into our world around us. We are able to build design into our homes, dwellings, lives, and landscapes. In essence, we see design for design's own special, esteemed, and ordained sake. It is a world of design, established in design, held together by design, and made for designers! Enjoy the moments we have been given!

About the Author

Rich Starshak has been a garden designer for over twenty-five years. He and his family purchased a two-acre piece of ground in 1996, which in essence was a weed field, a large tree, and a barn. They have since designed and built a mini-botanical garden complete with thirty-five individual garden areas including a 4,000–square foot ideas garden, a landscaper's challenge garden, a large organic family vegetable garden, hydrangea, hosta, sun, shade, topiary fun gardens, and more!

He has provided extensive complementary landscape designs for many homes, his community, businesses, churches, schools, and governmental offices. Through the years, Rich has created and developed his own mathematical and geometrical guidelines to apply to landscape design, holds workshops and teaches such design principles, holds multiple tours each year for the community and schools, and continues to provide guidance and direction for local landscape projects.

This writing is a culmination of those twenty-five years of designing and is intended to be a workbook for those who are either beginning or those who have been designing landscapes for some time. This material is intended to challenge how we design, how we conceptualize, and how we utilize and apply mathematical and geometrical principles into the process as we contemplate that perfect landscape design!

CPSIA information can be obtained
at www.ICGtesting.com
Printed in the USA
BVHW022240160222
629075BV00030B/1059